STICKS AND STRAW:

Comparative House Forms
in Southern Sudan and Northern Kenya

INTERNATIONAL MUSEUM OF CULTURES
Publication 13

William R. Merrifield
Series Editor

Jacqueline E. Bernhardt
Academic Publications Coordinator

STICKS AND STRAW:

Comparative House Forms
in Southern Sudan and Northern Kenya

JONATHAN E. ARENSEN

INTERNATIONAL MUSEUM OF CULTURES
Dallas, Texas
1983

© Summer Institute of Linguistics, Inc. 1983

Library of Congress Catalog No: 81–50907

ISBN: 0–88312–164–6
ISSN: 0197–3746

Cover design: David Beasley
Photos: J. E. Arensen

This title available from:

International Museum of Cultures
7500 West Camp Wisdom Road
Dallas, TX 75236

CONTENTS

List of photos vi
List of figures viii
Preface ix
Introduction 1
PART I - WESTERN SUDAN 9
    Mangayat 13
    Zande 21
    Shatt 30
    Bongo 35
PART II - CENTRAL SUDAN 41
    Dinka 45
PART III - EASTERN SUDAN 53
    Murle 56
    Didinga 65
    Toposa 71
    Lotuko 76
    Longarim 81
    Ik 85
PART IV - NORTHERN KENYA 93
    Turkana 97
    Shangilla 103
    El Molo 107
    Samburu 110
    Rendille 115
CONCLUSION 119
Appendix: Communications cited 125
Bibliography:
    References cited 129
    Sources consulted 132

Photos

Poles support the roof	18
Grass for thatching	18
Sun-dried mud brick walls	19
Mud-plastered pole floor	19
Pole benches	20
Framework of a temporary dwelling	20
Molding mud walls	29
End view of a rectangular house	34
A background of woven grass mats	34
A platform for storage	39
Pole walls chinked with mud	39
Square house with rounded corners	40
Contemporary stick-walled house	40
Temporary Dinka shelter	50
A house on an extended platform	50
A Dinka cattle byre under construction	51
Completed cattle byre	51
Murle dwellings	63
A single home	63
Highland Murle homestead	64
A Highland Murle house	64
Drying corn	69
Didinga permanent dwellings	69
Women's temporary shelters	70
Contemporary Didinga house	70
A millet granary	74
Toposa sleeping house	74
A Toposa village	75
A Toposa cook house	75
Village on a terraced hillside	79
A platform tower in a Lotuko village	79
Lotuko house under construction	80
A cylindrical house	83
A fenced village	84
Turkana homes	100
A Turkana settlement	101
A high-domed dwelling	101
Temporary sleeping quarters	102
Houses overlooking Lake Rudolph	105
Shangilla house frame	105

Contents

Roofing material 106
The El Molo island village 109
A Samburu desert house 113
A multiroomed highland house 114
Replastering the house 114
Rendille dwellings 117
Moving day 118

Figures

Fig. 1.	Map of region under study	xii
Fig. 2.	Precipitation and vegetation regimes	6
Fig. 3.	Ethnic areas and elevations	7
Fig. 4.	Language classification chart	8
Fig. 5.	Southwest Sudan	10
Fig. 6.	Mangayat village	15
Fig. 7.	Straggling Zande homestead	23
Fig. 8.	Circular homestead	24
Fig. 9.	Mud house for senior wife and grass house for junior wife	25
Fig. 10.	Boys' sleeping house	26
Fig. 11.	Kitchen house	26
Fig. 12.	Nineteenth-century sleeping house	27
Fig. 13.	Borrowed house forms	28
Fig. 14.	Construction stages	28
Fig. 15.	Shatt decorated dwelling	32
Fig. 16.	Mat-walled raised house	32
Fig. 17.	Two-story platform house	32
Fig. 18.	Bongo homestead	37
Fig. 19.	Nineteenth-century Bongo houses	38
Fig. 20.	South central Sudan	42
Fig. 21.	Nineteenth-century Dinka house	48
Fig. 22.	Types of cattle byres	49
Fig. 23.	Southeast Sudan	54
Fig. 24.	Floor plan of Murle house	60
Fig. 25.	Murle migration stops	61
Fig. 26.	Position of houses in a Murle homestead	61
Fig. 27.	Didinga homestead	68
Fig. 28.	Ik dwelling built on a slope	88
Fig. 29.	Private compound	89
Fig. 30.	Ik village	90
Fig. 31.	Northwest Kenya	94
Fig. 32.	Turkana homestead	99
Fig. 33.	Samburu settlement (Spencer 1965:18)	111
Fig. 34.	Side view of a Samburu house	112
Fig. 35.	Layout of a Samburu house	112

PREFACE

Most of my life has been spent in East Africa where my parents are missionaries. I spent my first thirteen years in Tanzania near Lake Victoria and then went to high school in Kenya. After college in the United States I returned to teach near Nairobi for three years. During these years I traveled extensively, learning about East African cultures and environments. I became interested in southern Sudan and northern Kenya since these were two places I had not visited, but had had contact with missionaries whose stories of this area intrigued me. However, Sudan was closed to the outside world because of the civil war, and getting into northern Kenya was also difficult because of disturbances on the borders with Ethiopia and Somalia. So it was not until the 1970s that tensions eased and there was a possibility of my working in these areas.

After the civil war ended in Sudan in 1972, I heard that the Summer Institute of Linguistics was looking for two people to make a linguistic survey in southern Sudan. My wife and I applied for the job, and after special training were assigned to the specific area of southern Sudan and northern Kenya. In Sudan we worked directly under the Minister of Education since our goal was to travel throughout the southern three states of Bahr El Ghazal, Equatoria, and Upper Nile, and to collect language data. This was done in order to analyze the situation for purposes of literacy, and to establish criteria for choosing regional trade languages. My wife and I worked in seventy-seven language groups in southern Sudan, and later collected data on thirteen more languages in northern Kenya. We covered about ten thousand miles, never staying in one language area more than a few days.

We followed a set procedure with each language. This entailed taking the Swadesh 200-word list and also 120 grammatical constructions. Also, short narratives were taped and used in neighboring languages to test bilingualism. By taking the same data in each language, it was possible to compare word lists and grammatical constructions and to see the relationships between languages. Our results came out very similar to those of Tucker who did his work in this area during the 1930s and 1940s.

Not knowing what we would find, it was difficult to choose a specific study topic before the trip. As we traveled we therefore made general observations on a wide variety of topics including population, environment, lifestyle, subsistence focus, houses, dress, and weapons. Usually we added to our observations by asking questions about many of these topics, although in some areas this was not possible where we were unable to communicate with any of the indigenous population.

It was during the latter part of the trip that I actually chose house forms as the specific topic for this study. I gradually became interested in differences in house forms from community to community, and started trying to find reasons for these differences. After my decision to write on this topic, I observed houses even more closely, asked questions about them, and took photographs specifically for this book. Asking people why they built a certain way seldom helped since they usually responded that this was the way they always did it. Simple observation was often the best way to gather data on this topic.

Research was later done in various libraries including the University of London, University of California at Los Angeles, University of Washington, and Central Washington State College. The data presented in this book represent only a small part of that gathered during the entire trip.

Although the subject of house forms from this area has been carefully researched since the field trip, literature on this subject was found to be inadequate. This study, therefore, is only an overview of house forms from this area of Africa. Where there are gaps in the information, it is because there was not time to gather it on our trip, and because it is not yet available in the literature. I hope in the future to be able to add more information to that presented in this study.

I would like to express my thanks to the many people of Sudan and Kenya who were helpful to me as I gathered this information. I

Preface

also appreciate the help from my graduate advisors, John Ressler, Linda Klug, and Paul LeRoy for their assistance in putting the material into organized and readable form. Most of all I would like to thank my wife Barbara who assisted me as I collected these data. Her company and help on the many arduous trips made the experience truly enjoyable.

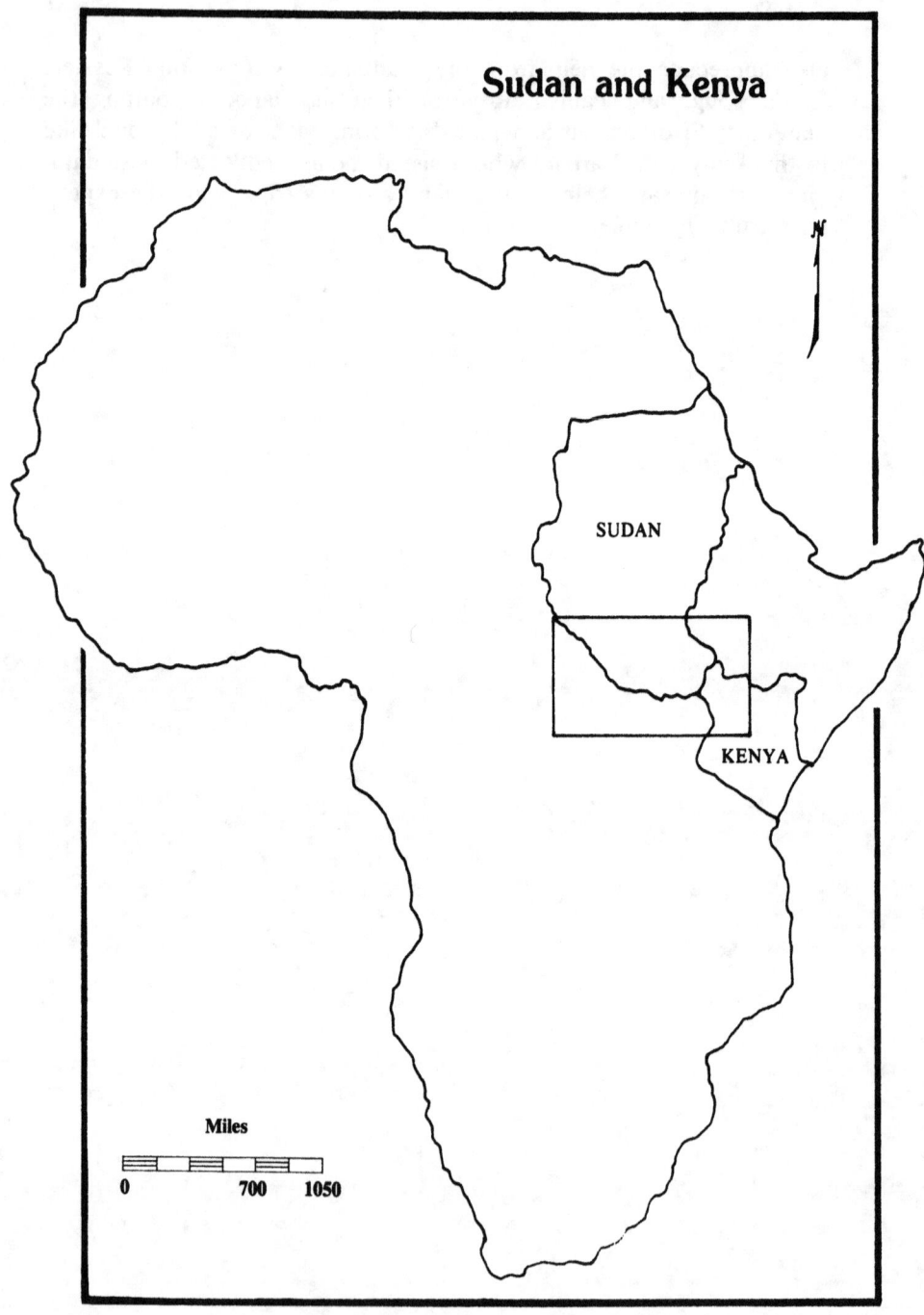

Fig. 1. Map of region under study

COMPARATIVE HOUSE FORMS
INTRODUCTION

Southern Sudan and northern Kenya are inhabited by a large number of ethnic groups living in diverse environments and having different lifestyles. These groups build their houses in a limited number of forms that vary according to sociocultural factors, local environment, subsistence focus, history, and linguistic affiliations. This book discusses these different house styles and the people who build them. The purposes of the discussion are twofold.

The first purpose is simply to describe and document the house forms that exist in this area. All of the houses included here can be classified as indigenous structures. *Indigenous* does not necessarily mean that the buildings are simple or primitive, but rather that the houses are built by members of an indigenous society. Rapoport (1969:8) defines indigenous housing as having "very few building types . . . with few individual variations, built by all."

These houses are well adapted to the builders' way of life and environment. By studying indigenous housing it is possible to gain insights into the lives of the people who build them. "The intimate relationship between the society and its shelter is self-evident" (Oliver 1969:27). This is reinforced by Obot (1974:85) who states, "Because people live in houses their beliefs and behavior are manifested in the form."

Indigenous buildings are visible proof of how man has adapted to the physical world around him, as well as to internal sociocultural pressures. Gardi (1973:29) states that "houses are the purest reflections of lifestyles." This is probably an architect's overstatement, but nevertheless shows the importance of documenting indigenous house forms before they disappear.

The second purpose of this book is to study various house forms and formulate reasons as to why people build their houses in the ways they do. This will be done by comparing house styles from sixteen communities and analyzing the cultural and physical conditions that make demands on house forms. Rapoport (1969:8) states that houses cannot be studied in isolation from the people who build them. It will therefore be necessary to describe the cultural settings of individual house forms. This will necessitate supplying some anthropological data on each ethnic community since their culture, means of subsistence, and social patterns all have an important influence on house form. Geography, history, and linguistics of the various communities are discussed when they have a bearing on the house types.

Some hypotheses

Building a house involves enclosing space. The method in which this space is enclosed determines the house form (Rapoport 1969:104). In southern Sudan and northern Kenya, however, the living space usually involves a larger space than just the dwelling. The house itself may be enclosed and private, but much of the living space is outside and shared with others. This living space will be included as part of the dwelling since the two are inseparable.

There is a tendency to try to find one primary factor which determines all house forms. Obot lists six different determinants, each of which has been put forward as a primary factor by one unspecified theorist or another. He states that no one of these is the primary determinant, although all do have some bearing on house forms (Obot 1974:84).

The first determinant is climate, and although this does have an important impact on house form, there are numerous exceptions. For example, people such as the Ona of Tierra del Fuego have dwellings that are almost totally inadequate for providing warmth under the nearly Antarctic conditions (J. B. Jackson 1961:28).

Materials, construction, and technology have also been presented as primary determinants, but most scholars now dispute this. "Materials are rarely a determinant of form, but rather are an influence on decisions of coping with social values and constraints" (Dickens 1974:25).

Introduction

Site is the third determinant, but "it seems impossible to predict house forms and settlement patterns based solely on ecological site" (Obot 1974:84). Defense, religion, and economics are the final three determinants. Although all of these do apply in certain situations, they are not universal to all house forms.

All of these six determinants are important and are applicable in various situations, but no one of them is the most important in all house forms. One should not "attribute all varying forms to a single cause" (Obot 1974:84). Prussin (1969:6) sums up the situation by stating that "it is evident that there is no simple explanation for the existence of a particular architectural form."

There is one important factor that is omitted from the determinists' viewpoints: the sociocultural impact upon house forms. According to Obot, this actually has a closer relationship to house form than the previously mentioned determinants. "The physical qualities (of a house) are interactions between sociocultural factors implicit [sic] and those environmental determinants of site, climate, and defense" (Obot 1974:85). The understanding of any structure must be accompanied by a knowledge of the "cultural milieu that has generated it. A cultural milieu is the product of forces acting within it as well as of those external to, but acting upon, it" (Prussin 1969:2). Prussin goes on to give examples from Ghana where the climate, materials, and economy are virtually identical, but the various ethnic groups build differing house forms. It is obvious that some determinants play greater roles than others in different societies. "It is in this respect that the sociocultural model is superior; it does not presuppose that only one primary factor affects the village, but that there are other factors responsible for any structure" (Obot 1974:85).

This book presents various house forms of southern Sudan and northern Kenya and shows how some of the sociocultural and physical factors have an impact on them. These sociocultural and physical factors are usually so interwoven and complex it is virtually impossible to discover all the forces at work in creating each individual house form.

A broad generalization covering all house types is rarely applicable, but the following hypothesis seems to be consistent in southern Sudanese and northern Kenyan house forms. Indigenous house forms appear to reflect the subsistence focus of the people who build them. Therefore I hypothesize that, for this region, *the primary influence on house form is the subsistence focus of the group that builds it.* This hypothesis does not exclude the many other factors that also operate; however, subsistence focus does have an important bearing on all of the house forms under study. I shall discuss this problem further as the various house types are presented.

Two secondary hypotheses are also presented. The first is that *history has an impact on house forms*. The second is that there is a relationship between house form and a people's *linguistic affiliation*. These secondary hypotheses will be discussed where pertinent, and conclusions will be given in the summary to the book.

The region

The geographical area under study begins on the border of Sudan and Central African Republic, and extends across southern Sudan into northwest Kenya (see map, fig. 1). Approximately ninety distinct peoples live within this area; so certain ones have been selected for this study which offer a variety of lifestyles and house forms.

The region includes many diverse environments such as woodland savannah, forest, swamps, plains, mountains, and deserts (see map, fig. 2). All of these environments support people who have adapted to the special environmental conditions. The book is divided into four major sections which correlate with the four major ecotypes. These sections are herein called Western Sudan, Central Sudan, Eastern Sudan, and Northern Kenya. The environments within each of these is fairly consistent except for eastern Sudan which is quite diversified.

Southern Sudan and northern Kenya are interesting from an anthropological and linguistic viewpoint since most of the peoples have retained their traditional cultures and languages. Much of this region remains one of the least-known areas of Africa (Nelson 1973:9).

The peoples studied can be broken down by subsistence focus into three categories. The first category consists of the agriculturalists, who live primarily in western Sudan and in the mountains of eastern Sudan. Their subsistence focus is food derived from their gardens, although many of them hunt and fish to supplement this diet. They normally live in scattered homesteads near their fields, and their houses are strong and permanent.

The second category consists of the nomadic peoples who live primarily in the desert areas of Kenya where agriculture is difficult. These peoples live on the milk and blood of their livestock, and therefore must keep moving in order to find sufficient grazing for their herds. Houses are small, and parts of them are carried from location to location.

Most of the peoples of central and eastern Sudan fall between the first two categories. These groups are seminomadic with a combination of livestock and gardening for subsistence. In all cases, however, they consider their cattle to be of primary importance, and so their cultures are focused on the herds. These groups maintain large permanent villages, but the younger men and sometimes the younger women are often gone for weeks at a time following the cattle herds and sleeping in temporary shelters until they return to the village.

The strictly hunting and gathering peoples no longer exist in the area under study. Because of government restrictions on hunting, these groups are now basically agriculturalists. Some groups still have those who are skilled as hunters and beekeepers, but the number of such individuals is decreasing.

The subsistence patterns of all these peoples are influenced in a definite way by the environment in which they live. An indigenous people cannot grow gardens in the desert, nor can it herd cattle in tsetse fly infested woodland. Lifestyles are well suited to environments, and house forms reflect adaptability (see figure 3 for the location of the peoples under discussion).

The history of most of these groups has been passed on orally, and only in recent years has some of it been written down. History in this study is of the origins, wanderings, and wars of the various peoples. In some groups little is remembered of their past, while in others a more extensive history has been passed on from generation to generation. When history has an impact on the house form, it will be discussed in the appropriate sections.

In order to show relationships between house forms and language affiliations, it is necessary to show how languages are related to each other. Figure 4 presents a language classification of the groups included in this study. The classification is a combination of those used by Greenberg (1963) and Tucker and Bryan (1956).

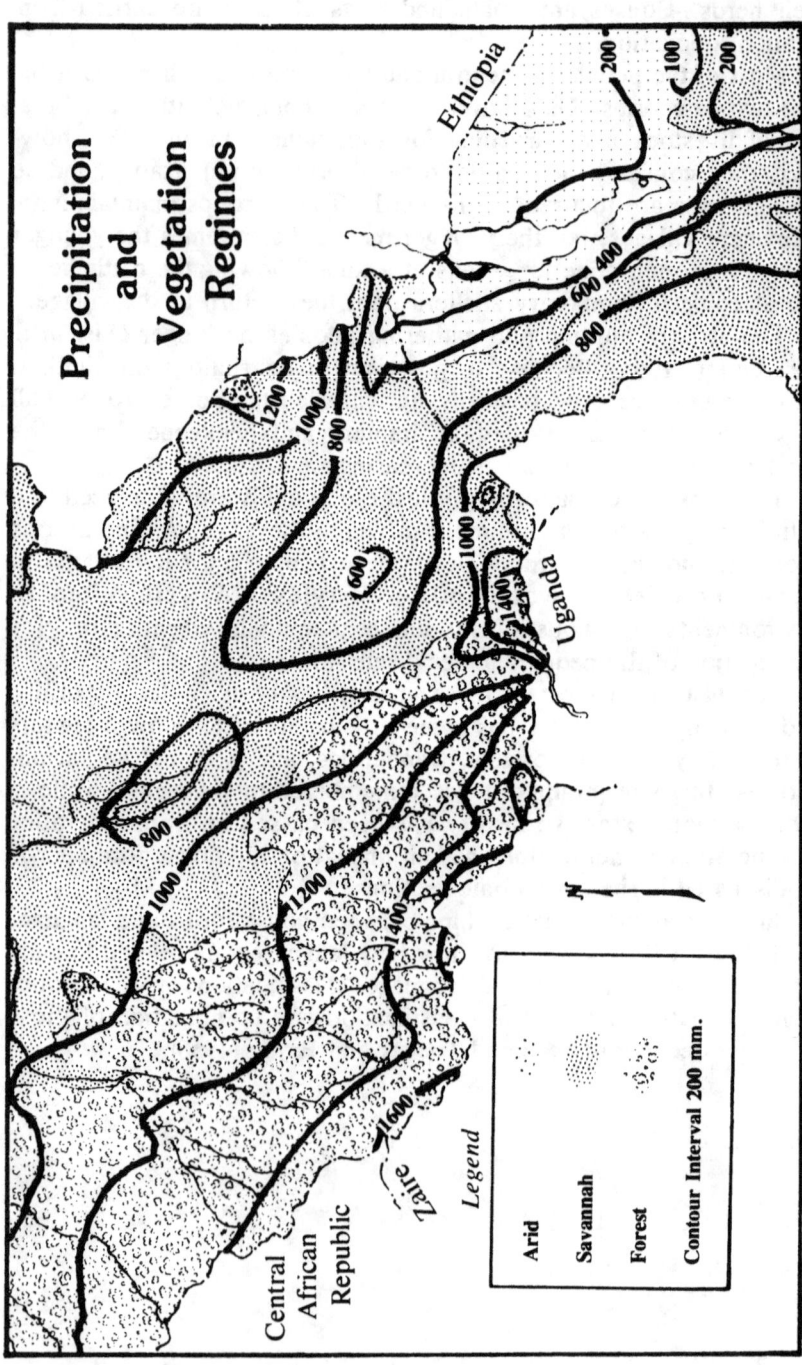

Fig. 2. Precipitation and vegetation regimes

Introduction

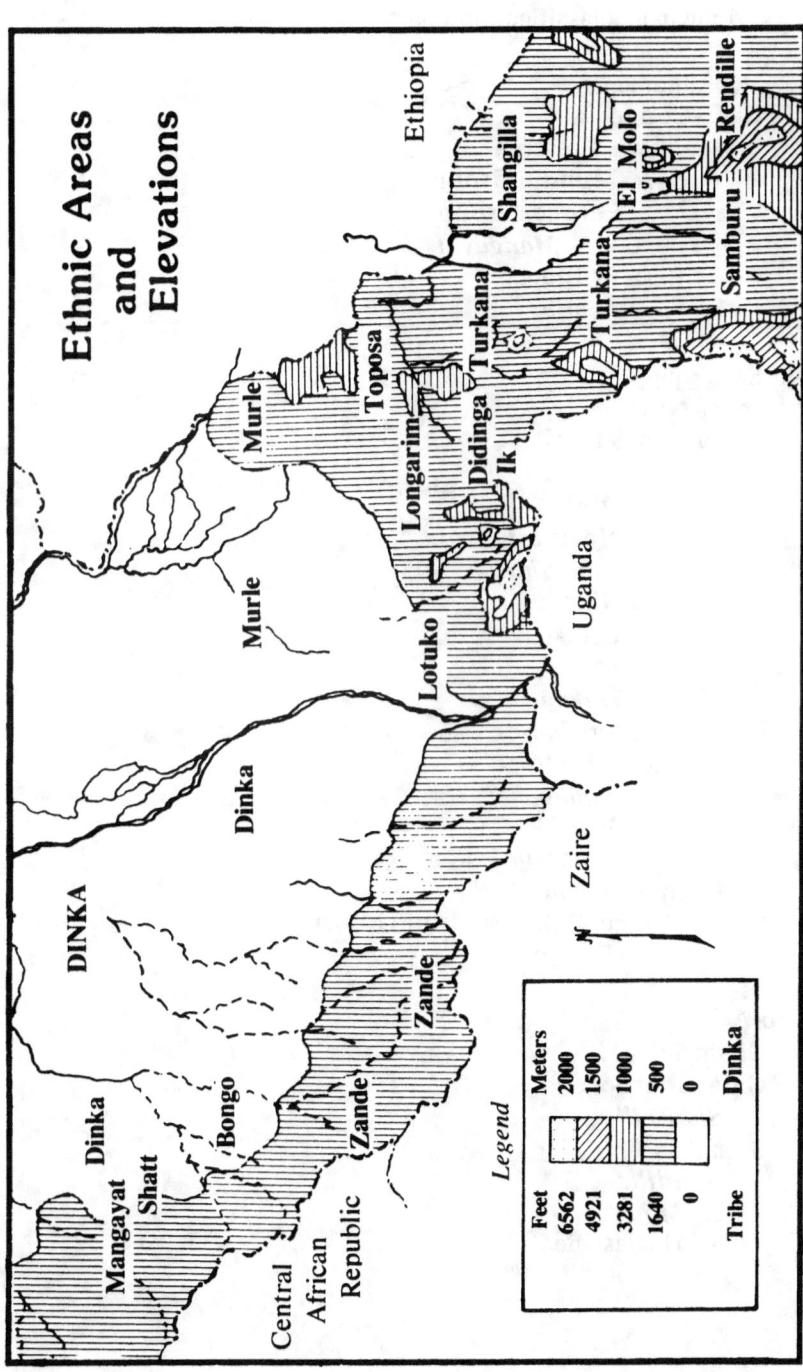

Fig. 3. Ethnic areas and elevations

Fig. 4. Language classification chart

Niger-Kordofanian
    Niger-Congo
        Adamawa Eastern
            Sere-Mundu Group
                Feroge Group
                      Mangayat
            Eastern Branch
                Zande

Nilo-Saharan
    Chari-Nile
        Eastern Sudanic
            Nilotic
                Dinka
                Northern Lwo
                    Shatt
            Para-Nilotic
                Lotuko
                Toposa
                Turkana
                Samburu
            Didinga-Murle
                Didinga
                Murle
                Longarim
        Central Sudanic
            Bongo-Baka-Bagirmi Group
                Bongo

Afro-Asiatic
    Cushitic
    Galaba-Arbore
        Shangilla
    Somali
        Rendille
        El Molo?
    Ik — Unclassified

PART I

WESTERN SUDAN

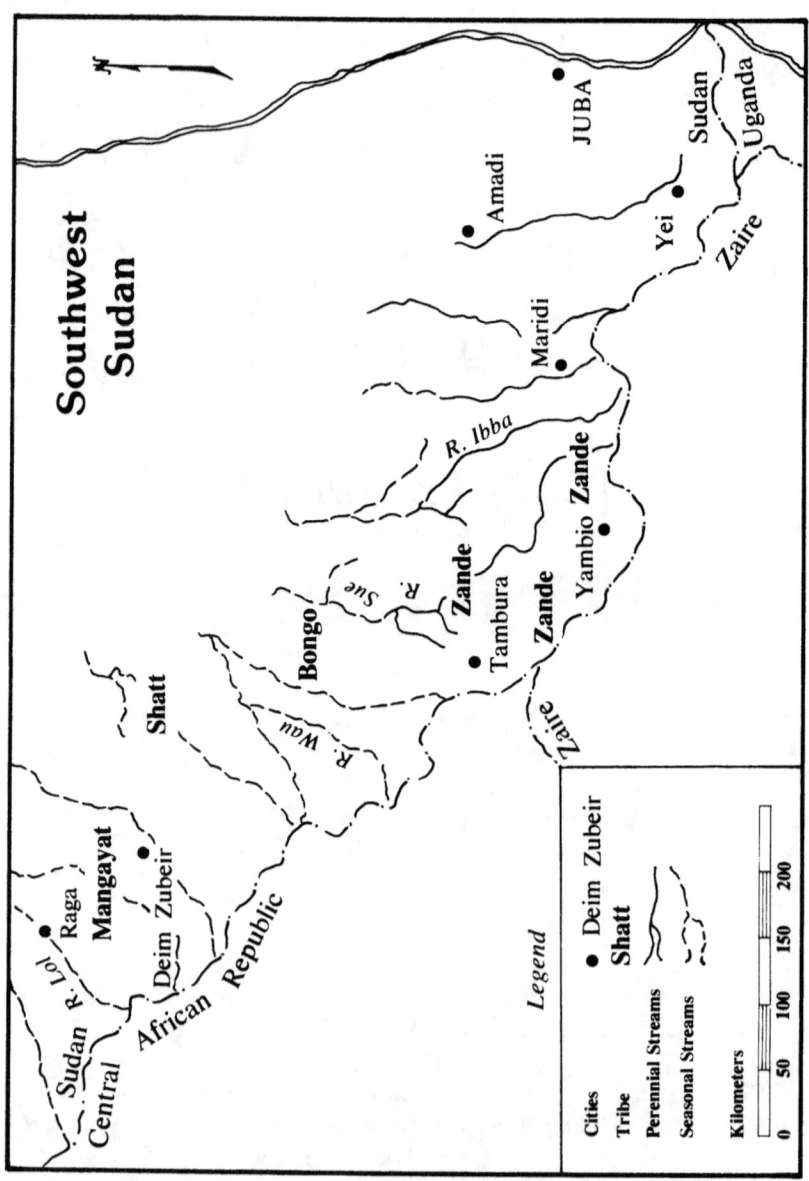

Fig. 5. Southwest Sudan

INTRODUCTION

Over the entire area of western Sudan, the environment is fairly consistent. It is generally flat with only a few gently rolling hills in some regions. The soil is basically laterite catena (Sudan Survey Dept. 1974), with ironstone composing some of the higher areas and black clay in the river areas. Here and there within the region are small granite hills which protrude abruptly from the surrounding area.

Western Sudan receives between twelve hundred and sixteen hundred millimeters of rain per year (Barbour 1961:47), and small perennial streams are numerous. The continental divide of Africa forms the border between Sudan and Central African Republic. This divide is not a mountain range, but only a slight ridge of about a three-thousand-foot elevation. All water to the west of the ridge flows to the Congo River and thence to the Atlantic. All water to the east of the divide flows in many small rivers through western Sudan, eventually merging with the Nile and flowing north to the Mediterranean. These rivers give peoples living in the area adequate water all during the year.

The vegetation is fairly uniform over all of western Sudan—a combination of woodland and savannah. The larger vegetation is mostly *Anogeissus-khaya-isoberlinia* deciduous trees (Sudan Survey Dept. 1974). These trees average about twenty feet tall and grow separately, so they do not supply a constant cover of shade. Between these trees grows the tall grass for which Africa is famous. When this grass reaches its full height of six to eight feet in the dry season, it makes visibility low and travel difficult. It is then burned by the men so that the area may become more open for hunting and traveling. The southern part of western Sudan along the Zaire border is better watered, and in recent times the vegetation there was canopy forest. Much of this forest has been cut down and cleared for gardens, so this area is rapidly becoming woodland savannah. The abundance of trees and grass over all of western Sudan is an important factor in providing building materials for the houses of this region.

The temperature during the day is often around 100° F. The humidity is not as high as in central Sudan, but is still uncomfortable. Temperatures do not fall much below 60° at night. The altitude to the far west is a little higher because of the continental divide, but not enough to lower the temperatures appreciably. Houses therefore are generally built to stay cool rather than to provide warmth.

The rainfall in the area is enough to help the people grow good gardens. The people living in this area are all agriculturalists who do some hunting to supplement their diets. The woodlands breed tsetse flies (*Glossina morsitans*) that infect cattle with sleeping sickness (*nagana*), so this environment is unsuitable for stock raising. Wild game, however, are immune to the disease, and many species live in the woodland savannah. Hunting is practiced by all groups to some extent, but hunting is often difficult because of the heavy cover and the tendency of game to stay scattered.

MANGAYAT

The Mangayat live near a granite hill called Jebel Zakka in western Sudan. They are the westernmost of all of the peoples studied. Their villages are about midway on the road between Deim Zubeir and Raga. They are a small group which in its entirety is composed of only 565 people (oral communication, Mangayat chief, Jan. 1975).

The Mangayat and three other small groups, the Feroge, Indri, and Togoyo are all linguistically classified in the Feroge language group. A turbulent history has brought the Mangayat into contact with many other peoples, with the result that they are now multilingual. Most of them speak Ndogo, the language of the schools, and Kresh, the trade language of the area. Banda and Feroge are also spoken. Those who have traveled know Zande and Pidgin Arabic. In spite of this multilingual situation, the Mangayat continue to maintain their own language and speak it among themselves.

Their history is complicated, so it is not easy to acquire a complete or accurate picture. Buga is the original name of the Mangayat who claim that they originated in some small rocky hills about twenty miles west of their present villages (oral communication, Mangayat chief, Jan. 1975). Although they are now agriculturalists, there is evidence that when they lived in these hills they were cattle people (Santandrea 1953:257). These cattle were the stocky, humped type similar to those now owned by the Toposa in eastern Sudan. There is no good explanation as to where the cattle came from, since no neighboring groups are known to have ever possessed cattle. Moreover, there are no cattle of this particular strain even remotely close to the Mangayat Hills.

The Mangayat were always few in number and would retreat to their hills whenever threatened. In 1890 the Njalgulgule dominated the Raga area. The Mangayat, feeling threatened, retreated to their hilltops where they entrenched themselves with stored food and water. Knowing that they could not fend off the Njalgulgule by themselves, they sent a message to the Zande in the south asking for assistance. The Zande responded and defeated the Njalgulgule. After the battle, the Zande then turned on the Mangayat (Santandrea 1953: 256). Traditions vary here. Some say that Mangayat held the hills by rolling large stones down upon the attacking Zande. Other stories claim that the Mangayat were defeated and some of the Mangayat were taken captive by Zemoi and his Zande warriors. In Zandeland these Mangayat were so well treated that some who were left in the hills voluntarily moved south to live among their relatives. Close ties were maintained between those in the Mangayat Hills and those in Zandeland, and eventually most of the captives escaped and returned home. There are supposedly some Mangayat still living among the Zande since they enjoy the elephant hunting in that region.

After the Zande influence ebbed in Raga, the Njalgulgule and Feroge again attained dominance. The Njalgulgule people were allied with Arab slave traders and would capture people from weaker groups, selling them as slaves to the Arabs. It was during this period that the Mangayat came in close touch with the Feroge language. The Mangayat have no ethnic ties with the Feroge since these came from Kordofan in the north, but the languages have definite similarities which may have developed during the period of Feroge dominance.

The British were the next to make their appearance in the area, and under the colonial government many of the smaller groups were relocated near newly built roads. It was under the British that the Mangayat left their hills and moved to their present location on the road.

The Mangayat are presently agriculturalists with most of their gardens being planted with millet. As with most Sudanese peoples, this grain is stored in raised granaries until needed. The millet is then pounded into flour, mixed with water, cooked, and eaten in the form of a thick porridge. The villages in which they live are shaded by mango and papaya trees which supply fruit during the dry season. The Mangayat presently keep no livestock other than a few chickens.

Mangayat

They have given up much of their old culture, but not their language. This is true of all thirteen peoples of the Raga area. These groups have been so displaced and mixed together that at the present time their culture is quite homogeneous. The British, during the colonial period, relocated many of them along the roads, introduced new crops, and began an education system. The Roman Catholic church introduced a new religion and western dress. Then during the recent civil war, the Sudanese government moved entire groups into the towns for their own protection. Since the war, some of these peoples have chosen to remain in these towns rather than return to their former locations. The Mangayat were chosen for this study because they are a typical example of many of the small groups of the Raga region.

Houses in this region have been standardized. Different groups no longer have unique house styles but build in the present standard forms. These houses have some relics of the old culture, but have now incorporated new building techniques learned from the Arabs and the British. The houses of the Mangayat are typical of all the houses in this region.

The Mangayat do not build their houses around a central courtyard, nor do they fence them in, although ancient house sites indicate that they may once have done this. Houses are situated in a random fashion along the road. If people are related, they may put their houses close together, and a hard trampled courtyard may form between the houses, but this does not seem to be planned.

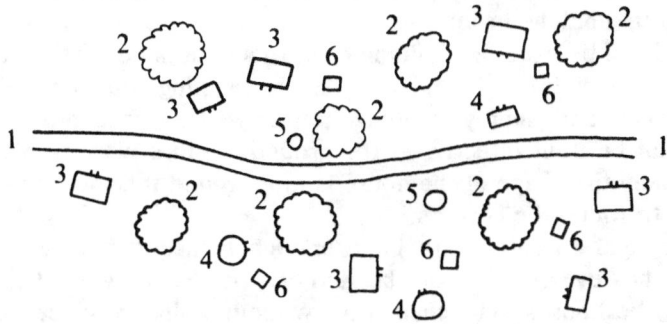

Fig. 6. Mangayat village

1. Road
2. Mango trees
3. Large rectangular brick houses
4. Small houses on stilts
5. Sun shelters
6. Granaries

The walls of most of the houses are built of sun-dried mud bricks mortared together with soft mud. Most houses are rectangular rather than round, since it is difficult to build the traditional round houses with rectangular bricks (see photo). The method of using bricks for building was introduced by the British and the Catholic missionaries, and has since been incorporated into the Mangayats' own building technique.

A framework of poles is erected to hold up the thatched roof. The load-carrying elements for this framework are not usually the mud walls, but these long, forked poles which extend to the ground outside the mud walls. Since the roof does not sit on the walls, it is possible to extend the eaves of the roof so that rain will not wash away the mud walls.

The roof is thatched with long bundles of grass tied to the framework. Thatching starts at the eaves and works to the cap so that higher layers overlap lower ones and will not leak when it rains. Dickens observes: "Thatching allows the rain to run right off and still gives the roof a breathing quality for much needed ventilation" (1974:26).

Some of the Mangayat still prefer raised houses and have devised a way of making mud-walled houses on platforms. A sturdy platform of wood is built three to four feet off the ground. This is built in a square, then the mud bricks are laid around the circumference of the platform. The rough wooden platform is plastered with mud to form a smooth floor. The framework for the roof is either fastened directly to the walls or to long poles that run all the way to the ground to hold up the thatched roof.

Mud can be used for building even though it is not first made into bricks. A small house can be built by making mud of a doughy consistency and simply molding it into walls. These molded mud walls can be built directly on the ground or on a wooden platform, but usually the shape of the house is more round than square since it is easy to round the corners.

Mangayat dwellings are large enough to accommodate a whole family; however, much of the activity of the village takes place outside the houses. Thatched roofs without walls are placed around the village on raised poles. Benches are made by setting poles into crotched sticks driven into the ground to a comfortable height. These benches are built under the sun shelters and under the mango trees. Such shady areas are where the people spend most of the day when they are not working in the fields.

Mangayat

Mangayat granaries are not enclosed as among many Sudanese peoples, but instead consist of a raised, unroofed platform. Millet is laid on top of the platform and exposed to the sun.

Temporary homes are sometimes built by the Mangayat. A square framework of sticks is built, and grass tied to it to form the walls and the roof. These houses are used only until more permanent mud-walled houses can be built.

Mud-brick walls are not traditional among the southern Sudanese, and rectangular houses are also rarely built. This house type is similar to those of the Arabs from northern Sudan. The fact that peoples of the Raga region are now building rectangular houses instead of their former cylindrical ones is an indication that their recent history has destroyed much of their old culture. In this case their entire way of life has been so disrupted that there is no desire to return to their old ways. Instead, they have decided to copy the more dominant Arabs, and have adjusted their house forms accordingly.

Cylindrical houses with conical roofs are the traditional houses among most agriculturalists in tropical Africa. These are built from available materials and are not only cool and comfortable but durable enough to last a number of years. Since years may be spent in a dwelling, generally a great deal of time and care goes into its construction. Houses are always situated within walking distance of the gardens. The present rectangular houses, though of a different material and of a different shape, still meet the same requirements as the former cylindrical houses.

Western Sudan

POLES SUPPORT THE ROOF. Small Mangayat houses are elevated on wooden platforms. The weight of the roof is held by poles running to the ground from a frame under the roof.

GRASS FOR THATCHING. The primary material used for thatching is grass. It is carried in large bundles to the building site.

SUN-DRIED MUD BRICK WALLS. Handmade, sun-dried mud bricks are laid on an elevated wooden platform as walls for a dwelling.

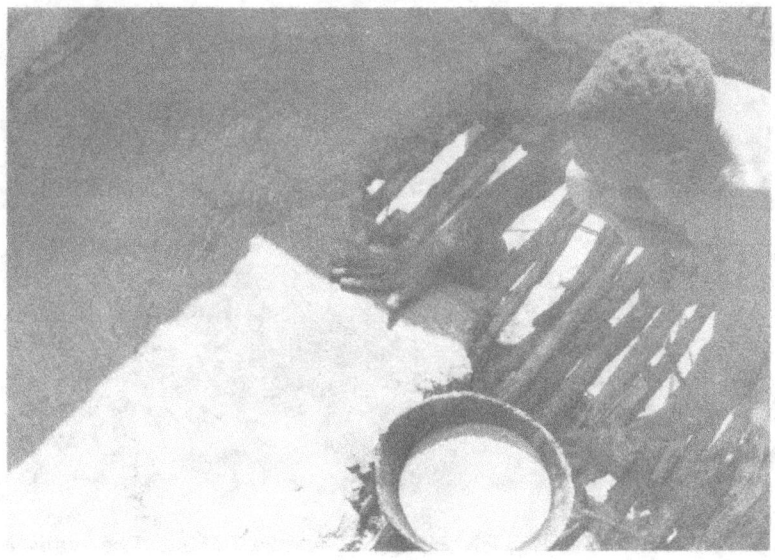

MUD-PLASTERED POLE FLOOR. The pole floor of an elevated house is plastered smoothly with mud.

POLE BENCHES. The Mangayat people socialize while seated on their pole benches in the shade.

FRAMEWORK OF A TEMPORARY DWELLING. The walls of many Mangayat houses are made of a framework of poles and sticks. This may later be plastered with mud or covered with long grass.

ZANDE

The Zande are a large group with a population of over 600,000. They inhabit all of southwestern Sudan and extend far into Zaire and Central African Republic. At the last census (1955) the Zande population in Sudan was about 212,000 (Nelson 1973:74); more recent figures are unavailable.

Zande is the dominant language in this area of Africa, and most smaller groups in this region have learned to speak it. Zande is used in the schools, and a number of books have been translated into this language.

The original name of the Zande was Mbomu, named after a river in northern Zaire. This river is reportedly the original home of the Zande. The name Zande was supposedly later given to them by the British. The history of the Zande and their migrations north into Sudan is well documented by Evans-Pritchard (1971) in his book *The Azande*. The Zande people formed one of the finest fighting forces in all Africa. During the nineteenth century, under brilliant war captains, they conquered a large portion of central Africa.

The Zande formed three political classes. The top class were the *Avangaro* who comprised the chiefs and leaders in battle. The second class was composed of the original Zande clans. These were called *Ambomu* and were the warriors. As the Zande conquered smaller groups, they absorbed them into their ranks, as a class called *Auro* (Evans-Pritchard 1971:Introd.).

Most battles among African peoples were mere skirmishes, with each individual making his own decisions. Under the *Avangaro* chiefs, the Zande army became well organized and disciplined. Leaders were responsible for certain numbers of fighters, and these leaders made definite battle plans before attacking. Battle strategy was quite sophisticated in that it involved techinques such as pincer movements and separate armies attacking from opposite directions. Spears and throwing knives were the primary fighting weapons (Bicknell 1972:43, 44). Since smaller groups could not put up a united front, Zande armies went on long trips conquering everyone they could find. There are many references to the Zande eating their dead enemies, but the subject of cannibalism is still debated. The Dinka name for the Zande was Nyam Nyam supposedly because of the way they smacked their lips when eating human flesh. Cannibalism seems to have been limited to isolated groups; most Zande today deny having had any part of it (oral communication, Kparabatiko, Dec. 1974).

The main key to Zande growth and success was that, after conquering another people, they incorporated many of them into their own ranks. These groups were quickly absorbed and would soon be speaking Zande and fighting for the Zande in their battles. By this method of absorption, the Zande continually swelled their ranks and became harder to stop. Eventually the Zande became a mixed group comprised of many different peoples with only the *Avangaro* chiefs maintaining their ethnic purity.

The Zande conquered all of southwestern Sudan and began making forays as far north as Raga. Eventually they engaged the Dinka in central Sudan. Since the Dinka were a large, warrior tribe, a long protracted war seemed probable. The new colonial government intervened, and the Zande withdrew to southwestern Sudan; however, they continued to make raids until the British sent a regiment down to the Zande area. At this time the whole Zande organization was disintegrating internally, so the British had little trouble in removing Chief Yambio from power and setting up a colonial administrator.

One of the first major problems the new colonial government had to face was how to stop the sleeping-sickness epidemic which was decimating the Zande population. Sleeping sickness is spread by the tsetse fly which breeds in thick bushes near water. The government decided to move the Zande into large concentrated villages. The bushes around these villages were cleared so that the tsetse fly could not reproduce. Also it was easier to give medication to people in concentrated villages than in scattered homesteads. This move into villages was initially resisted by the Zande who did not like living close together; however, the move was carefully supervised and was successful in solving many of the health problems.

Zande

During the recent civil war many of the Zande left Sudan and went to live with the Zande in Zaire and Central African Republic. Since the end of the war they have been moving back into Sudan by the thousands. At the present time they are building many of their homes near the roads which offer transportation to the towns and trading areas. This has had an influence on their settlement and house patterns and will be discussed later in this section.

The area in which the Zande now live was once covered with canopy forest and receives more rainfall than the area north of them. The Zande are an industrious people who have cleared much of this forest and planted their gardens. They produce a wide variety of crops including millet, maize, manioc, sweet potatoes, arrowroot, eleusine, sesame, and various types of fruit. They are one of the few peoples of Sudan who raise more food than they can eat. This surplus is sold in local trading centers. Both coffee and cotton are also grown as cash crops. The markets in Zandeland have more variety than any other markets in southern Sudan. There is a cash-oriented economy among the Zande, most of whom purchase western clothing and other status symbols such as watches and bicycles.

The Zande are unable to keep livestock because of the tsetse fly; however, they have a craving for meat and so hunt in the forests. The major hunting techinque is netting: nets are set in the forest and small game is chased into them, where it is speared. The Zande are reported to eat almost anything that moves. Their favorite meat is a voiceless breed of dog which they raise and fatten as a delicacy.

Before the Zande were moved by the British, original homesteads were scattered throughout the forest. The advantage of having scattered homesteads was that each could be built near its gardens.

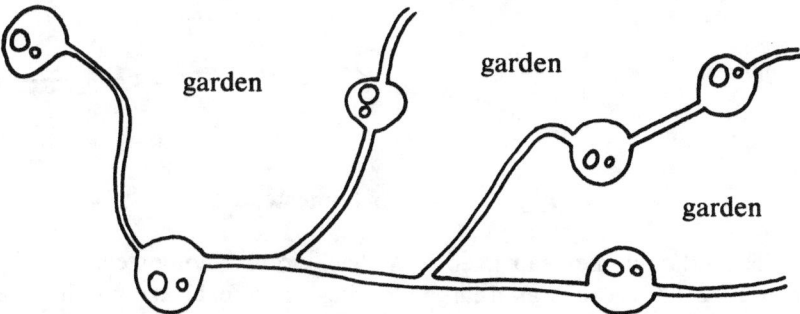

Fig. 7. Straggling Zande homestead

There were basically two kinds of homesteads. The first is referred to by Evans-Pritchard as "straggling homesteads" (Seligman 1932: 498). In this system each woman had her own small clearing in the bush. The clearing contained her house and granary and was surrounded by her gardens. These clearings were from one hundred to three hundred yards apart and were connected by footpaths winding through the bush from one clearing to another. A woman and her children would live in each clearing. The husband would stay with whichever wife he wished for the night but did not have his own house. Each woman had her own garden near her house in which she raised sweet potatoes, arrowroot, and bananas. The men in the homestead would plant their fields on the outskirts of the whole homestead and there they would raise crops such as maize, millet, peas, and sesame.

The benefit of this straggling homestead was that people were near to their gardens and could care for them better. Since the region was once canopy forest, the soil quickly leaches out if exposed for a long period of time. So the Zande rotate their crops, allowing certain areas to lie fallow in order to keep from using up the fertility of the soil. Even so, the fertility of the soil is limited, and the Zande tend to move every two or three years (Singer and Street 1972:6).

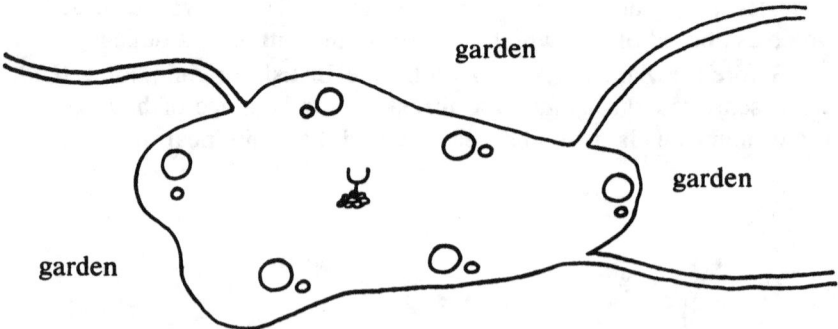

Fig. 8. Circular homestead

The other homestead used was the "circular homestead" (Seligman 1932:499). This was a large clearing where each woman had her house and granary on the perimeter of the same clearing. The clearing was not surrounded by a fence, but by the women's gardens.

Zande

Each woman had her garden close behind her house, and the men's gardens were farther out in the forest. Each homestead was a self-sufficient unit and each house owner had certain rights. Each adult not only owned his or her own house but also the use rights to gardens, beds of wild mushrooms, termite hills, and hunting areas.

The original dwelling houses of the Zande were cylindrical with conical roofs. These houses were well built, the walls being made of solid mud. The roof sat directly on the mud walls and was thatched with grass. These houses took some time to build because of the thick, heavy walls. When a man became married for the first time, he built a substantial mud house for his first wife (Evans-Pritchard 1974:54). Subsequent wives often had to be satisfied with a bell-shaped house built entirely of grass. The cone-shaped framework of poles was set directly on the ground, and the grass thatch reached all the way to the ground. This formed a roomy, comfortable house, but eliminated building of mud walls.

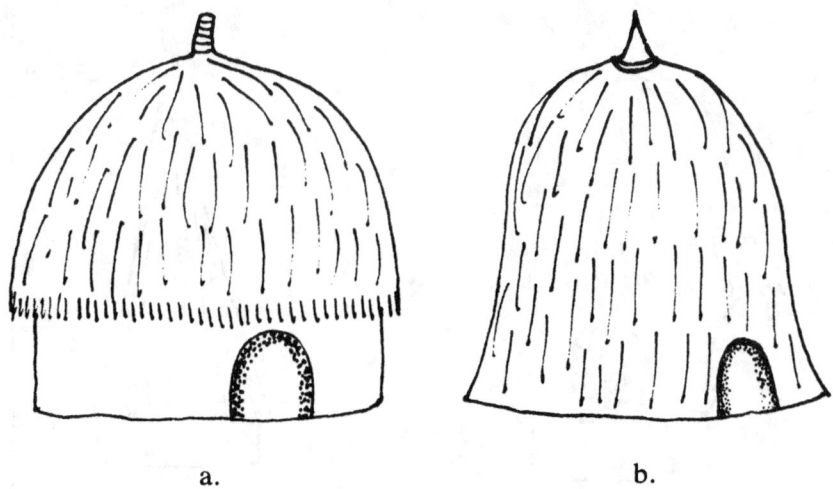

Fig. 9. Mud house for senior wife (a) and grass house for junior wife (b)

Back in the days when the *Avangaro* ruled the Zande, some of their houses were very artfully made. Most Zande houses were built with a practical purpose in mind, but the ruling class was in a position to have buildings emphasizing esthetic values. The Zande claim that the present houses are smaller and less impressive than the old ones (Evans-Pritchard 1974:182). The following three examples were seen by Schweinfurth (1875:Tab. XI) when he traveled through the Yanbio area. The first is a small sleeping house used by boys of the upper class. The walls are carefully molded out of clay with decorative patterns around the base and the wooden door. The solid structure is to protect the boys from nocturnal animals, and the wooden door could be braced shut from the inside. Tall-roofed kitchen houses were built for the women. Not only were they graceful looking, but the tall roof allowed the smoke from the cooking fires to rise and stay out of the women's eyes. The women not only cooked in these houses, but also lived in them. The same basic technique of building was used except that the frame for the roof was built much higher before being thatched with grass.

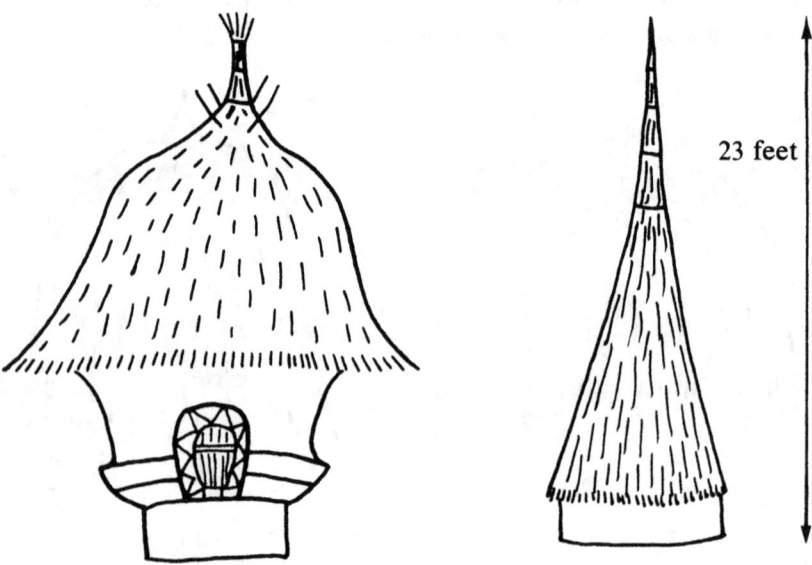

Fig. 10. Boys' sleeping house   Fig. 11. Kitchen house

Zande

The third example by Schweinfurth was a beautiful dwelling with a double peak. The double peak was of no practical value, but was built entirely for its esthetic value.

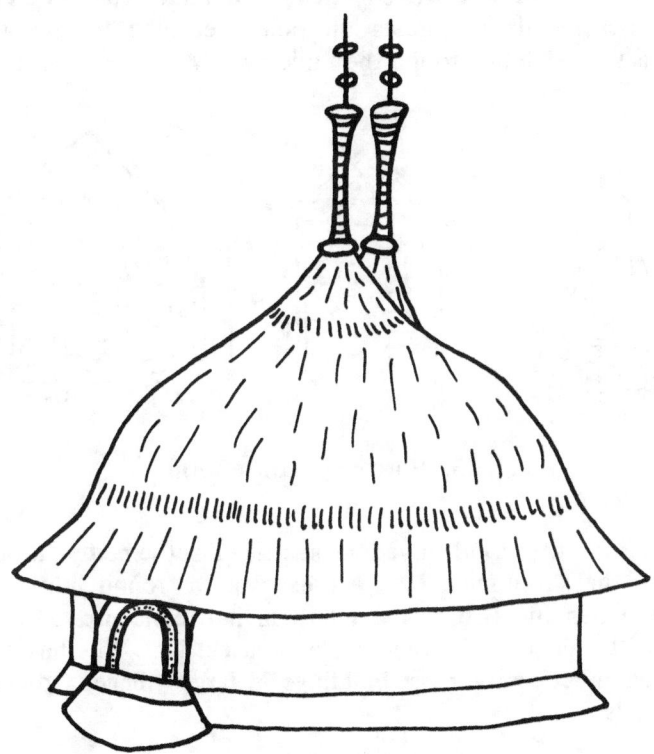

Fig. 12. Nineteenth-century sleeping house

During the Zande conquests when smaller groups were absorbed into the Zande culture, they brought some of their old culture patterns with them. When these groups built their new homes in Zandeland, they built them in their traditional form. The result of this amalgamation of cultures is that the Zande no longer have a single house form, but a multitude of house forms from various areas of central Africa (Hodgkin 1951: 108–9). Each person builds the type of house that suits his personal taste.

Most Zande still use the round house with a conical roof, but rather than building solid mud walls, they build the walls of wattle woven around the frame and chinked with mud. This style seems to have come from groups in the south of Zandeland. Other houses are built on raised platforms—a style probably learned from groups to the north and east. Some of the larger dwellings are built by making a five-foot wall of interwoven sticks and mud. The roof extends beyond these walls and rests on poles reaching to the ground, forming a verandah all around the building.

Fig. 13. Borrowed house forms

As long as the Zande lived in scattered settlements throughout the bush, they continued to use these varied, round house styles; however, when the British moved them into concentrated villages, they were taught to build rectangular houses. Now this has become a common practice for most buildings in large villages, towns, and on the roads.

Fig. 14. Construction stages

The walls of these rectangular houses are made of mud—either of sun-dried bricks or molded mud. Two heavy, forked poles are placed in the middle of the dwelling to hold up the central ridgepole. A framework of poles is then built between the walls and the ridgepole, and the weight of the roof is carried by both the central poles and

Zande

the mud walls. This framework is then thatched smoothly with grass. These large rectangular houses are often divided into several rooms and are inhabited by a husband, wife, and their children. Christianity has had a strong influence on many of the Zande and most of them are now monogamous, so it is no longer necessary to have separate houses because of multiple wives.

The environment in which the Zande live makes few demands on the Zande house form. The basic physical reason for houses is protection at night from animals, shelter from the rain, and shade during the day. The forest around them supplies them with an abundance of natural building materials. Within this setting it is possible for the Zande to build a large number of house types which would all meet the physical and social requirements. The basic house form decided upon was a round house with a conical roof, but history has a strong influence on house styles, as can be seen among the Zande. During the conquests many new forms were adopted; the British introduced a new concept of rectangular houses. The result is that now the Zande build houses in a great variety of styles. The ultimate decision on house form seems to depend mostly on the degree of acculturation or simply on the personal preference of the builder.

MOLDING MUD WALLS. Some Zande houses are built on elevated platforms and have walls made by molding soft mud into the desired shape.

SHATT (THURI)

The Shatt comprise between three thousand and five thousand people who range over a large area between Wau, Deim Zubeir, and Raga. Their language is closely related to that of the Jur Luo who live east of Wau, but the Shatt lifestyle and physical characteristics are quite different.

As a people the Shatt are proud of their heritage and traditions, but their history is vague and often very confusing. There are two theories as to their origins (Santandrea 1968:60). One theory states that the Shatt are the remnants of a group called Luel which once lived in an area north of Wau but are now extinct. Some of these Luel, a Nilotic people, may have moved west and intermarried with an Arab people. After various battles, some of these people moved north and disappeared, and others moved south into the present Shatt region. These people retained their own Nilotic language, but through intermarriage with the Arabs they acquired new customs, lighter skin color, clothing, and amulets.

The second theory states that the Shatt originated in the north in Kordofan. At the present time a small Shatt community still exists in Kordofan who claim blood ties with those in the south, although the languages are completely different. This second theory claims that some of these light-skinned peoples moved south, intermarried with the Luel, and learned the Nilotic language. The Luo name for the Shatt is Thuri which is close to the Luo word *turu* (white man). This name is thought by some to prove northern origins. Regardless of which theory one accepts, it is obvious that the Shatt have had close ties with the Luo to their northeast and probably originated in that area, mixing with Arab peoples at some point in their history.

Shatt (Thuri)

Their more recent history consists of a lengthy wandering period (oral communication, Shatt chief, Jan. 1975). The Shatt have always been a small group which was never really united, so they were pushed from area to area by stronger peoples. The Njalgulgule eventually pushed the Shatt into the region in which they live today. Upon the arrival of the British, the various peoples withdrew to their own territories and were stopped from extending control over their neighbors. At this point the Shatt found themselves in possession of more than five thousand square miles. Since most of the population lives on the road, much of this region is virtually uninhabited and is the private hunting territory of the Shatt.

The Shatt were known as hunters who specialized in killing elephants. The weapon used in these elephant hunts was a large spear up to twelve feet long with a two-foot blade. This spear was not thrown, but was thrust overhand into the elephant's chest. Normally small bands of hunters consisting of five to ten men would attack an elephant. Some of the hunters would attract the elephant's attention while others worked in close enough to thrust their spears. Occasionally a man would kill an elephant by himself, and then would be considered a hero in his village (oral communication, Shatt chief, Jan. 1975). These elephants were the chief source of food; the tusks were traded for ornaments, metal, and clothing.

Recently elephant hunting has been officially banned by the Sudanese government. This has caused a great deal of discontent among the Shatt, and some hunting still takes place; however, most of them have turned to agriculture. Their main crop is millet, which they plant during the rains and store in granaries for the dry months. They are also experts in keeping wild bees, and honey is used as a drink and for sweetening their food.

In past years they spent much of their time moving from place to place following the elephant herds. Now, because they have to tend their fields, they have settled in more permanent villages. When the Shatt were more nomadic they probably had small, simple dwellings, but no information has been forthcoming on this point. Their houses are now standardized and are similar to those of the other agricultural peoples with which they border. Building materials are readily available since they live in woodland savannah where there is an abundance of grass and trees.

A typical Shatt dwelling is round, with walls built of poles smoothly plastered with mud. The conical roof is thatched with grass. This house is built directly on the ground and has a hard-

Fig. 15. Shatt decorated dwelling.

packed dirt floor. Some of the Shatt use the outside walls as space for their artwork where they paint geometric designs and scenes of past elephant hunts (Santandrea 1968:153). This house form is among the most common among the Shatt, and is a typical form used by many peoples of Africa.

The Shatt also build houses raised off the ground on wooden poles. This may be a style learned from the neighboring Dinka since

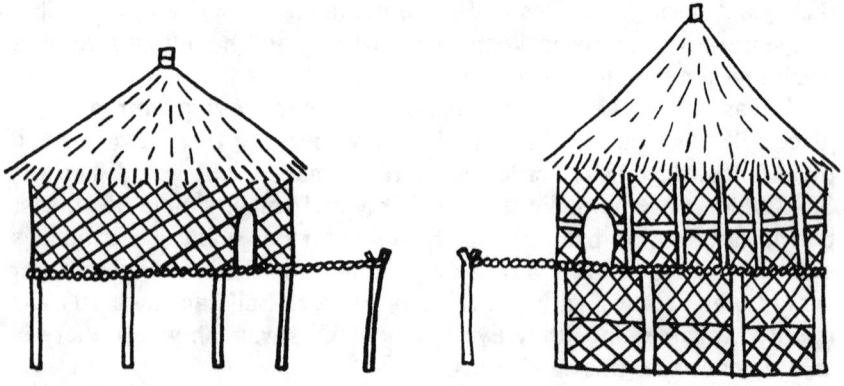

Fig. 16. Mat-walled raised house

Fig. 17. Two-story platform house

Shatt (Thuri)

it is similar, although smaller and more fragile. A platform is built on poles about four feet above the ground, and a round house is built on this platform. The walls are roughly plastered, then these are covered by a thick woven mat. The area underneath the platform is used as a shady sitting area or a kitchen. In some houses a woven mat is also placed around the bottom of the platform, forming a private room; in effect creating a two-story house. The benefit of having the house up off the ground is that the elevation provides safety from animals and snakes, while the area under the house provides a cool place in which to spend the heat of the day.

Recently some of the Shatt along the road have forsaken the traditional round house style and are building mud-brick houses in a rectangular shape. These buildings are similar to the rectangular houses built by the Zande and described in the previous section. The only significant difference is that sometimes the roof is extended in front of the house to form a large porch, and the bricks on the end of the building extend all the way up to the peak of the roof. This type of house is obviously not one of the original house forms, but has been adopted in recent years through contact with other peoples.

In large villages the Shatt houses are placed in a haphazard fashion around a central courtyard, and no strict rules of procedure are followed. Members of an extended family build in close proximity to each other, and a large woven fence is then placed around the perimeter for privacy. This fence is made from grass woven in a crisscross fashion, the same as the mats used around some of the houses.

Like many other small groups of western Sudan, the Shatt have moved around a great deal and have borrowed building techniques and house forms from various cultures with whom they came in contact. As a consequence the Shatt have no unique house form, their houses showing close similarities with those of their neighbors. Examples are the houses on raised platforms (that may have been borrowed from the Dinka) and the rectangular houses borrowed from the Arabs. The only practice the Shatt use which was not seen elsewhere is the weaving of large mats which are used in covering walls and in fencing courtyards.

END VIEW OF A RECTANGULAR HOUSE. Near the road, the Shatt are now building rectangular houses of mud bricks. A cross beam holds up the thatched roof, and a porch extends in front of the door.

A BACKGROUND OF WOVEN GRASS MATS. The Shatt encircle entire compounds with woven grass mats. They also use mats to cover mud walls of their houses.

BONGO

This once numerous people inhabits a sparsely populated area south of Tonj and extending all the way south to Zandeland. Some of the original explorers of this region estimated that the population was once between 100,000 and 150,000. Primarily due to decimation by slave traders and the Dinka-Zande war, the population of the Bongo is now somewhat less than five thousand. Accurate population figures are unavailable since the remaining Bongo live in the bush where no census has been taken.

The Bongo people originally moved into their present location from the south, somewhere in northern Zaire (Seligman 1932:465). This is obvious from their physical characteristics. They are short and light skinned and look quite unlike any of the tall, dark, and angular peoples to their north and east. The Bongo do have physical similarities with the Zande who also emigrated from northern Zaire.

Different waves of migrations took place out of Zaire, and one of the first of these moves was taken by the Bongo. They moved to the southern rain forests of Sudan where they found excellent hunting. Emigrations from Zaire continued, and the last and largest of these were the Zande. The Zande, who came as a well-organized and conquering army, pushed the Bongo north into a more inhospitable area between the Zande and the Dinka. The Zande kept extending their control until they began to fight a major war with the Dinka. The war was never completed because the new colonial government intervened and forced the Zande to withdraw to the south. The Bongo, who lived in the area separating the warring groups, lost many people; others were taken south as captives by the Zande. As with many Zande captives, they eventually intermarried with the Zandes and lost their own cultural identity.

During the 1870s the Bahr-el-Ghazal became a slave empire ruled by Zobeir Pasha and his son Suleiman (H. C. Jackson 1955:98). Over five thousand Arab slave traders roamed the area capturing people and either incorporating them into a slave army or shipping them up the Nile to be sold in Khartoum. Many groups fought fiercely against the slavers, and when captured would refuse to work but would pine away and die. The Arab slavers made a large initial attack on the Bongo who put up a united front. But the Bongo had no idea how to fight against firearms, so many hundreds were killed in this battle. After this defeat, the Bongo again split up into separate groups and moved back into the savannah woodlands. It was relatively easy for the Arabs to find these isolated groups and capture them. Bongo slaves soon became popular and in great demand, so the Arab slavers did their best to meet that demand. Only a few thousand Bongo out of over a hundred thousand were left when the British conquered the empire and abolished the slave trade.

The Bongo were once hunters, and some hunting is still practiced by the men. The area has many species of animals, but they are scattered, and in the tall grass they are difficult to locate and kill. The Bongo use spears, bows and arrows, traps, and nets to kill their prey. An old method of killing elephants was to place men with heavy spears in trees and then drive the elephants under the waiting spearmen. These men would then attempt to drive their spears into the spines of the elephants as they passed underneath them.

At the present time the Bongo do not rely heavily on hunting, but rather on their gardens to provide them with food. So the Bongo are essentially agricultural. Most of their crops consist of millet and corn which are grown in small gardens around homesteads. This grain is dried and stored on raised platforms exposed to the sun. The Bongo also collect wild fruit, nuts, and honey from the woodland around them, and in addition keep a few animals such as chickens, goats, sheep, and dogs (Seligman 1932:465).

The Bongo actually consist of a large number of small groups, each living in a separate area near a permanent water supply. There is no overall leadership exerted over these small groups, and each tends to go its own separate way. Each extended family has its own separate homestead; nearby homesteads are usually those of distant relatives. Because witchcraft and the casting of spells is greatly feared by the Bongo, they have a tendency to live as far from the neighboring homestead as possible so as to be out of reach of a

Bongo

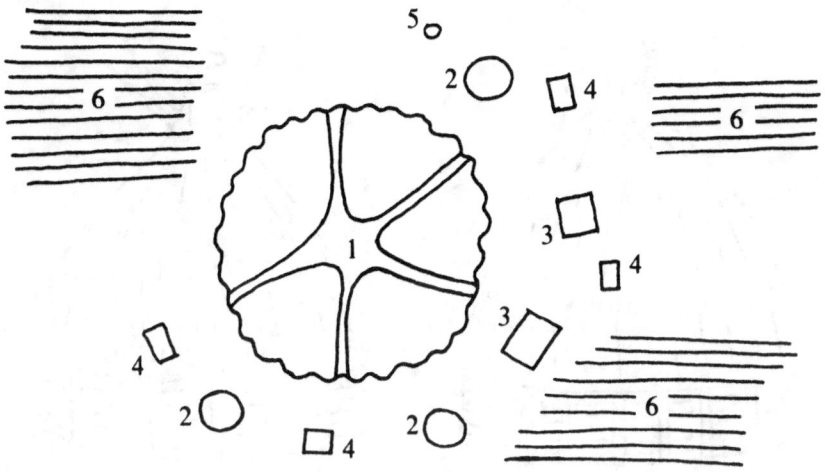

Fig. 18. Bongo homestead

1. Shade tree
2. Round dwellings built directly on the ground
3. Rectangular dwellings elevated on stilts
4. Raised granaries
5. Raised chicken house
6. Millet fields

spell. A Bongo priest from Tonj (oral communication, Father John, Jan. 1975) claims that most homesteads are presently placed about three miles apart. These homesteads consist of a few small houses usually placed around a large tree which offers shade to the inhabitants. Because of this practice of isolating themselves from other homesteads, it is rare to find a concentration of Bongo in any one area. This sparse population is of benefit to hunters since they are therefore seldom competing for the same game.

Schweinfurth was the first person to record information on the Bongo. In his book *Artes Africanae* (1875:Tab. VI) he presents illustrations of Bongo houses as he found them in the 1870s. These drawings show large, substantial houses placed on the ground. Walls were round and built with poles interwoven with sticks and plastered with mud. A conical frame for the roof was placed on the walls and thatched with grass in a smooth fashion. Four to eight of the roof poles were not cut but stuck several feet out of the top of the roof, seemingly for decoration. A large pad of grass was then woven and

Fig. 19. Nineteenth-century Bongo houses

used to cap the roof (Seligman 1932:466). The men would climb the roof and sit on this grass pad from which they would survey the surrounding area.

Present Bongo houses are similar, but there have been some changes. They still build some of their houses on the ground, but these are not as large nor as well constructed as those described by Schweinfurth, although they are of similar construction.

Many of the present houses are built on wooden platforms. The walls of molded mud are generally square with rounded corners; others are made with interwoven sticks plastered with mud. The roofs are thatched, but the traditional elongated poles have been shortened, so only a few inches protrude at the top. On most houses the grass sitting pad has been entirely eliminated, but a few have a small braided pad only a few inches in diameter. The women use the shady area under these raised houses as a kitchen.

The larger houses of past years may have been built when the Bongo had a more stable lifestyle. The present smaller houses are faster to build and may have evolved during the time the Bongo were attempting to avoid the slavers. Ornate tops on the roofs were probably an art form from a safer era when the society had some leisure time. These have since almost disappeared because they were of no real practical value. The raised houses were never mentioned by Schweinfurth. This house form may have been borrowed recently from the north and east where there has been a great deal of contact during the past fifty years.

A PLATFORM FOR STORAGE. The Bongo, like many others, store millet and other things on elevated platforms.

POLE WALLS ARE CHINKED WITH MUD. The Bongo build some houses directly on the ground. Walls are first built of poles, then the cracks chinked with mud.

SQUARE HOUSE WITH ROUNDED CORNERS. Walls made of molded mud have rounded, not square, corners. The crown of sticks and plaited cap are vestiges of a once large and ornate roof style.

CONTEMPORARY STICK-WALLED HOUSE. Some elevated houses never get beyond the stick-walled stage. The area under it is used as a shady kitchen.

PART II

CENTRAL SUDAN

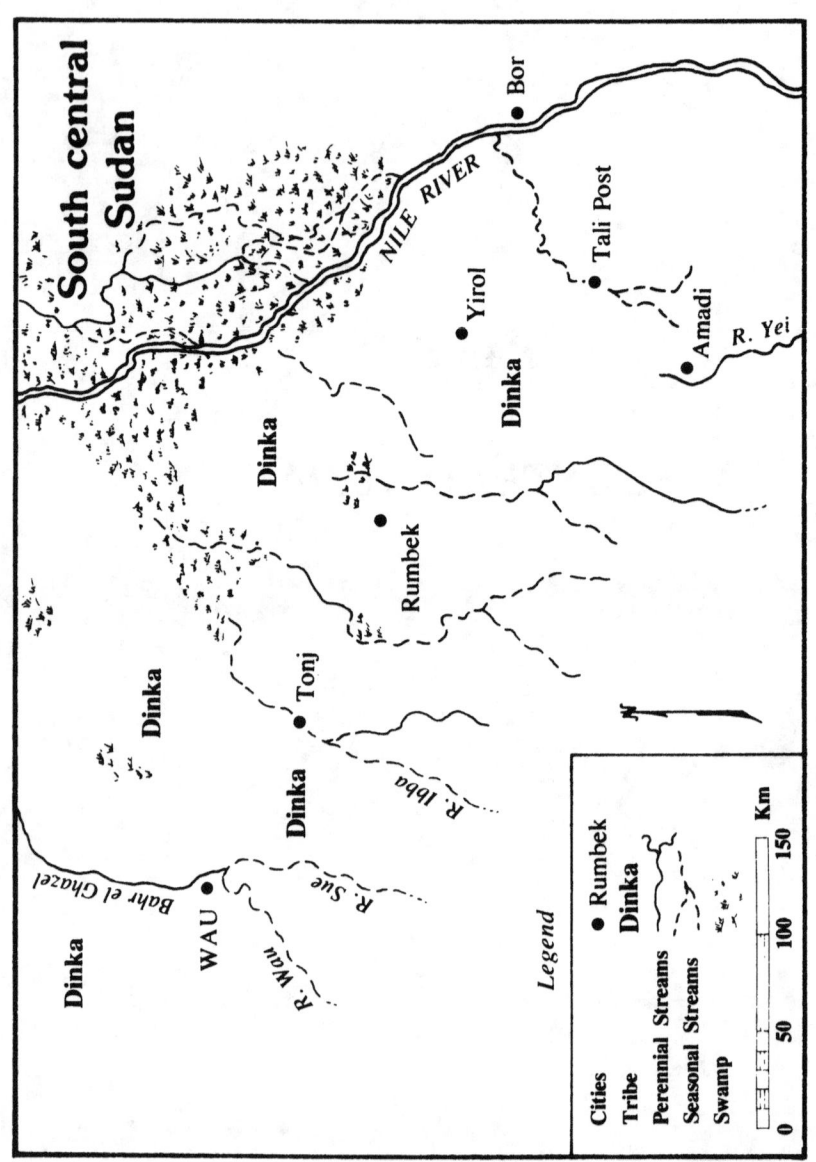

Fig. 20. South central Sudan

INTRODUCTION

Central Sudan along the reaches of the Nile River is primarily a land of excess water, swamps, and flood plains. The White Nile coming out of Uganda descends rapidly and has a strong flow. Once it arrives at Juba, the elevation is only about fifteen hundred feet, and the land flattens out. The Nile's flow is slowed, and the river begins meandering into many slow-moving channels. These channels eventually merge into a large swamp called the Sudd. This swamp is one of the largest in the world, covering about sixty thousand square miles. The river flow seems to come to a complete stop in the Sudd, and the channels are constantly changing course. During the rainy season the Nile rises rapidly, but when the excess water reaches central Sudan there are no banks to keep the water in the river channels. This water spreads out into the plains surrounding the river, creating vast flooded areas. Since the land is flat, there is no place for this water to escape. Once the ground is saturated, this water may remain for months until it evaporates.

The soil over this entire area is black clay. It becomes exceedingly sticky when wet and has no firm subsoil. All roads built in these clay areas are completely closed for about six months of the year. Once the water has evaporated in the dry season, the clay gets very hard, and large cracks appear in the ground. These cracks are several inches wide and often three feet deep. The early explorers to this area had a great deal of trouble with their pack animals whose feet would often stumble into the cracks. This clay is good for agriculture, but is either too wet or too dry to cultivate effectively.

Vegetation in the swamp consists mostly of papyrus reeds. These plants grow together in huge masses, the roots entangling and forming a thick mat of vegetation which floats on the water. Other water plants also become entrapped in this mass, making at times an impenetrable barrier to boats. These masses of vegetation weigh many tons and can change position with the help of the wind and the currents. Often they block entire channels, making a virtual dam which forces the water to go elsewhere and flood other areas; so the entire area is in a constant state of flux.

The flood plains around the swamp are covered with grass, and higher ground above flood areas contains some hardy bushes and small trees. South of the central swamps much of the land is above flood level, and here the vegetation becomes woodland savannah similar to that in western Sudan. Even further south, however, there are flat areas along the river which are under water much of the year.

Temperatures in the Nile region usually range above 100° F during the day and have reached as high as 130° in the shade. This region is also humid because of the vast amounts of water evaporating from the river and swamp under the hot sun.

Hippopotamuses, crocodiles, and fish thrive in the swamps. Elephants also live here in large herds, often standing up to their chests in water for days at a time. Specialized antelope such as the Nile lechwe (*Kobus megaceros*) have learned to exist here since they can put their heads under water and hold their breath while feeding. The entire swamp is a paradise for water birds such as ducks, geese, herons, and egrets.

DINKA

The Dinka are by far the largest people of southern Sudan, with a total population of about 1,150,000 according to the Sudan census for 1955. They occupy a wide area of central Sudan around the swamps and flood plains of the Nile and extend down into the woodland savannahs (fig. 20). The Dinka are actually composed of over twenty-five independent groups, each with its own name, but they all acknowledge themselves to be Dinka (Deng 1972:1).

Twenty-eight different dialects have been found among the Dinka, some of which are so divergent that the speakers of any given dialect are barely able to communicate with other dialect groups. These dialects fall into four major categories: Bor, Agar, Rek, and Padang. The Padang and Bor are located in the north and east in the swampy areas, while the Agar and Rek live in the south and west where the ground is higher and more wooded. There is a good deal of mixing among groups and dialects, so it is often difficult to make clear distinctions.

The Dinka arise from Nilotic origins (Evans-Pritchard 1940:3), most anthropologists and linguists considering this part of Sudan to be the original center of the Nilotic peoples. "Up to the fifteenth century, all River-Lake Nilotes lived just south of the point where the River Bahr-el-Ghazal meets the Nile" (Cohen 1968:142). Although many groups have since split off and moved to other areas, the Dinka still live in the same region. They have remained relatively isolated from the outside world because of the inaccessible area in which most of them live. Therefore, Dinka culture is still intact and they live as they have for generations.

The world of the Dinka revolves around their cattle. These are lean and bony, with long curved horns. They are of an ancient breed similar to those seen in pictures of ancient Egyptian cattle. When a boy becomes a man, he is given an ox; then the new man and his ox are given the same name. As these oxen grow, their horns are artificially curved in opposite directions. The men sing songs and quote poetry to their favorite oxen, and for festive occasions they decorate them with tassels that are hung from their horns. Dinka have an extensive cattle-related vocabulary with individual color words for every shade or combination of colors possible in a cow. The dairy products of these cattle herds are the main diet of the Dinka. They will also eat the meat of a cow that dies, but will not normally kill cattle for their meat. Cow dung is dried and used for fires in areas where wood is scarce.

Since there are many cattle, it is necessary to keep moving them around in order to get enough grazing. The Dinka as a people, however, are not completely nomadic, but rather are transhumant. They maintain permanent villages on slightly higher ground where older people and children reside much of the year with some small herds of milk cows kept nearby to provide food. The men, boys, and younger women are on the move most of the year, living near the cattle in temporary camps.

The cyclical flooding of the Nile provides excellent grazing for the Dinka cattle. When the flood waters are at their highest, the cattle are moved well back from the flooded areas to higher ground, since the cattle get hoof diseases from standing in water (Evans-Pritchard 1940:57). The rain brings up new grass on this high ground which is good cattle feed for a few weeks. Then as the dry season sets in, the floods begin to recede. As this water evaporates and recedes, fresh new grass comes up, providing new pasture. By the time this pasture is eaten, the water has receded several more miles, and new grass is coming up in its wake. This process continues through most of the dry season, providing green pasture when most of Sudan is completely dry. These flood plains of grass, called the *toich* by the Dinka, are where the Dinka herdsmen spend much of the year.

The Dinka also practice minimal cultivation. People who stay in the permanent villages scratch up the soil and plant millet, but this is not a major part of their diet as it is with many other Sudanese. The further south into the woodland savannah the Dinka live, the more agricultural and less cattle oriented they become.

Fish are also a part of the Dinka diet during the beginning of the dry season. Fish are difficult to catch during the floods, but when the water starts receding, it leaves many isolated pools where the fish become entrapped. At this time the Dinka go on trips to catch and dry the fish. Most fish are caught in circular nets with weighted edges that are thrown out into the pools, trapping the fish inside. When the pools get small enough, there are often more fish than water, and then it is simply a matter of picking up the fish and killing them. Groups of people go on these fishing trips, living in temporary shelters and drying the fish on racks for future use.

The simplest structures which the Dinka build are the temporary shelters used when herding cattle or on fishing trips. Since the people are in a given area for only a few days, little time is spent building these shelters. Usually a few branches are cut, stuck in the ground, and loosely covered with grass. Sometimes mud is thrown on top of the grass to help hold it all together. In grasslands where there is no other vegetation, a cone of grass is built directly on the ground. The basic purpose of these shelters is to provide shade from the sun during the heat of the day and some feeling of protection from wild animals at night. These shelters are small, allowing only one or two people to crawl inside and lie down. There is no consistent form, and they are not built with care since the Dinka are not interested in spending time and labor on a shelter they will soon abandon.

Dinka dwellings are built in permanent villages situated on high ground above the flood line. They may consist of from three to twenty homesteads. These homesteads of extended families are laid out in a completely haphazard fashion, often along the banks of a river.

The houses themselves are well constructed and can last ten years or more (Deng 1972:6). They are round with walls about four feet high of wattle and daub construction. Resting on the walls is a conical roof thickly thatched with grass. Evans-Pritchard informs us that "building and repairs generally take place early in the dry season when there is plenty of grass for thatching and enough millet to provide beer for the helpers" (1940:65).

There is some variation in house types depending on the building materials available. In the wooded area of the south many houses are built on large wooden platforms, some of which may stand six feet high and reach forty feet in length. The house is built at one end of the platform, the other end being left open to be used for living space or for drying grain and fish. The height offers protection from animals and insects, and keeps the Dinka above the mud and water during the rains (Walton 1956:143). The space under the platform offers a broad shady area that is used during the day, while the house is used primarily for sleeping at night. In reality, these houses are two-story buildings with living space on the bottom and sleeping space on top.

The Dinka of the north live in an area with so few trees that not enough poles are available to build platforms. Their houses are placed directly on the ground and are of similar design to those described above.

Schweinfurth presents an illustration of a Dinka dwelling of the type he found in the 1870s (1875:Tab. 1). The house he described was larger than the present Dinka dwellings. The weight of the roof was held up not by mud walls, but by a large branched tree trunk inside the house. Thatching was done in a tiered style similar to the method used by the Toposa today. Two small antechambers were built at the entrance so that the house could be defended from enemies.

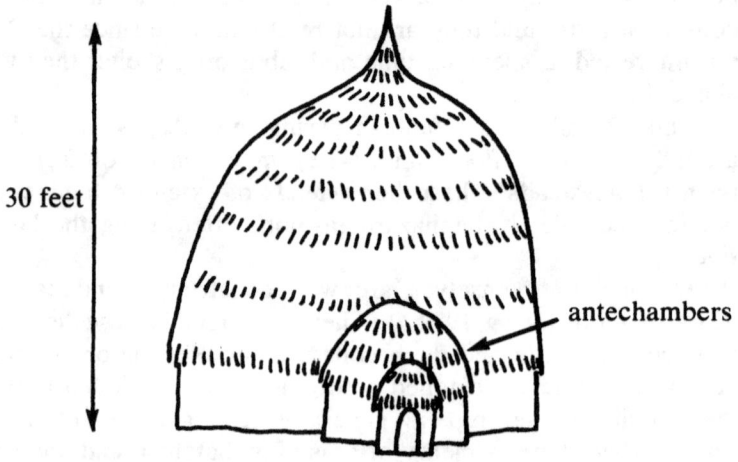

Fig. 21. Nineteenth-century Dinka house

Cattle byres are the largest structures built by any people of southern Sudan. They are basically oversized conical houses which can measure thirty feet in height and thirty feet in diameter. Dinka do not keep their cattle in kraals as do others, but from January to May they are kept outside, tied to individual stakes. Men sleep with

Dinka

them to protect them from lions. During the rest of the year, the mosquitoes are such a source of irritation to the cattle that they cannot rest, so they are brought into cattle byres (Evans-Pritchard 1940:31). The openings are closed, and a smoky dung fire is lit to keep down the mosquitoes. This dung fire provides the central meeting place for the men when they are in the homestead (Nelson 1973:130).

Two types of cattle byres are built. The first has a low strong wall around the perimeter, while the second consists of a roof coming all the way to the ground. The large roof is braced inside by tall poles placed vertically between the roof and the ground. The roof of both styles is smoothly thatched with short grass.

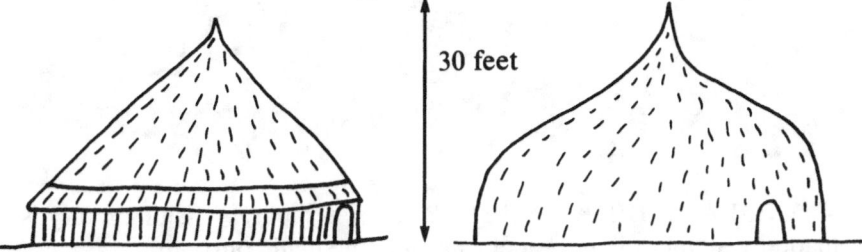

Fig. 22. Types of cattle byres

The subsistence focus of the Dinka is a combination of agriculture, cattle herding, and fishing. No one type of house can meet all the demands of their lifestyle; therefore, the Dinka build different house forms to fulfill different needs. Permanent dwellings are built on high ground near the millet fields. These houses are well constructed and comfortable, and are similar to those of agricultural peoples in western Sudan. The Dinka live in these houses during the rainy season while they clear and plant their fields. When the rains stop and the water recedes, the Dinka become nomadic in order to go fishing and to find new grazing for their cattle. They move out of their comfortable houses and build small, temporary shelters as they continue to move from place to place. These offer adequate protection during the dry season when there is no rain and few insects. The Dinka indicate that their primary subsistence focus is their cattle by building large byres to protect the herds from mosquitoes.

These various structures meet both the cultural needs and the environmental needs of the area in which the Dinka live. The house form being used at a given time of year reflects the subsistence focus of the people during that period.

TEMPORARY DINKA SHELTER. A temporary fishing camp is made by simply piling branches around a small courtyard.

A HOUSE ON AN EXTENDED PLATFORM. Where there are large trees, the Dinka build houses on extended platforms. The part not needed for the house serves for many family activities, as does the shady area beneath the platform.

A DINKA CATTLE BYRE UNDER CONSTRUCTION. Vertical poles support the roof of this large structure. The cattle dung piled in the foreground is for burning inside the byre at night to control the mosquitoes.

COMPLETED CATTLE BYRE. The pole framework is smoothly thatched with bunches of grass from top to bottom.

PART III

EASTERN SUDAN

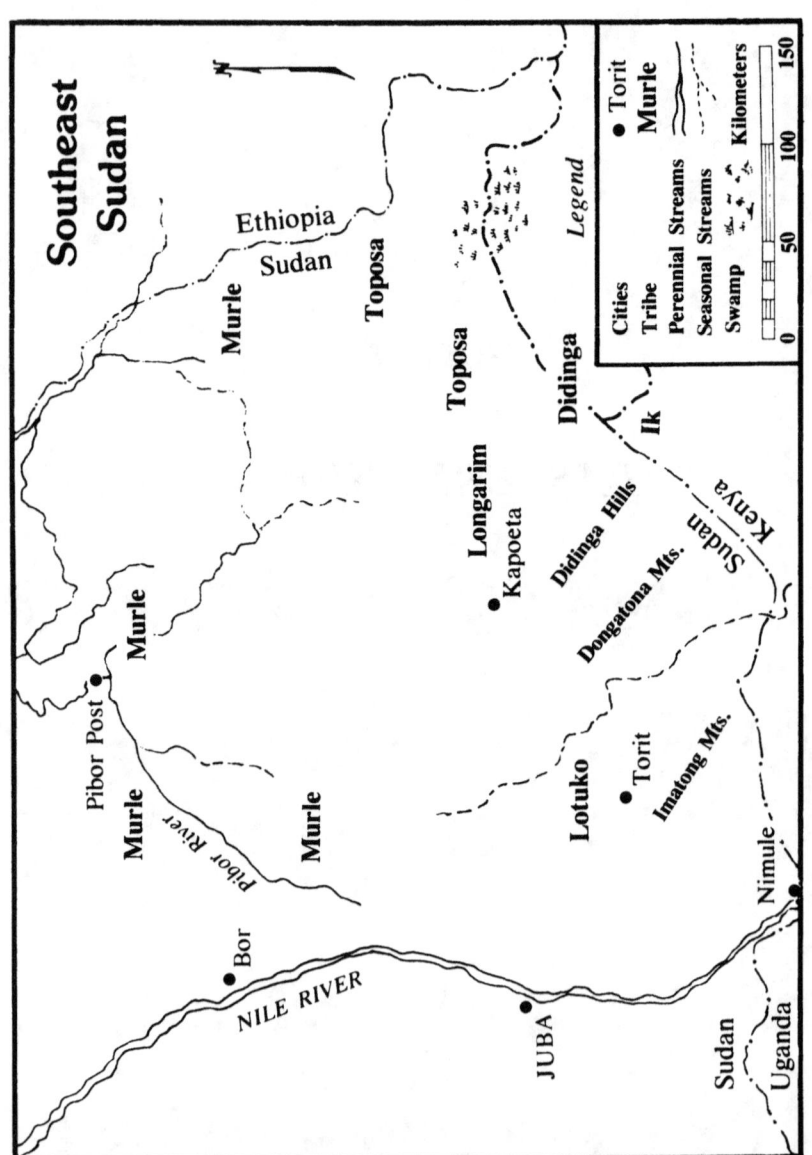

Fig. 23. Southeast Sudan

INTRODUCTION

Eastern Sudan has a variety of terrain. The central area is a vast flat region of black clay which turns into a morass during the rains and a dry savannah grassland the rest of the year. The last large herds of wildlife in Sudan roam this area. Along the Ethiopian border the terrain rises to the Boma plateau which reaches five thousand feet in elevation and has its own unique environment. South of Boma is a sloping plain descending into Kenya. The vegetation here is acacia bush traversed at regular intervals by dry, sandy watercourses. Along the Sudan-Uganda border are small mountain ranges, the Didingas, Dongotonas, and Immatongs being the largest. With the highest peak reaching eleven thousand feet, the climate in these mountains is much cooler than in the surrounding plains. The lowland region of the far south is woodland savannah, similar to that of western Sudan.

There are people living in all of these environments, and each group has adapted its lifestyle to the area in which it lives. Six of these will be dealt with here, and since the environment is different for each, they will be described separately in the following sections.

MURLE (BEIR)

The Murle number about forty thousand people. Their land includes a region extending from Ethiopia almost to the Nile River. The Murle are presently split into two groups living in different geographic locations and having differing lifestyles. The majority lives on the flat plains around Pibor Post and is referred to as the Lowland Murle. A smaller group lives on the Boma plateau near the Ethiopian border and is called the Highland Murle.

Both Highland and Lowland Murle speak the same language, which belongs neither to the Nilotic nor the Para-Nilotic family. A special category has been made for this language group. Linguistically they are closely related to the Didinga, Longarim, and Suri. The Didinga-Murle language group has never been adequately studied, and more research is needed in this area.

The history of the Murle has been handed down from one generation to another. They claim to have been created at a place called Jan in Ethiopia (Lewis 1972:19–23), from which in four stages they came to their present location. They first migrated down the Omo River to Lake Rudolf where a Murle village still exists today.

From Lake Rudolf they moved west to southern Sudan and settled near Kathangor. Here a split took place resulting in part of them moving to the Didinga Hills where they live today under the name Didinga. The rest moved north to the Maruwa Hills under pressure from the incoming Toposa. Here another split took place, with the majority moving west into the Pibor Post area, driving out the Dinka who were then living there. A small segment turned east at the Maruwa Hills and settled on the Boma plateau. They claim to have reached their present locations about four or five generations ago, which would be approximately 1880. In 1904 Captain Comyn of the British administration made the first official contact with the Lowland Murle by coming up the Pibor River when it was in flood (Lewis 1972:4). He impressed them with his firepower but was unable to bring the Murle under control, so in 1908 a British patrol set out to conquer them. A few minor skirmishes took place before the Murle leaders agreed to live under the British. Pibor Post was then built to supervise the area, but flare-ups between the government and the Murle continue until the present day.

The territory of the Lowland Murle is one of extremes which are often hostile to human survival. Rainfall is about nine hundred millimeters a year in the plains (Barbour 1961:47), but this flat area also receives the runoff from the Ethiopian mountains and Didinga Hills. During certain seasons of the year the whole land becomes a shallow lake. When rains are exceptionally heavy, the excess water makes life for the people and animals very difficult (Lewis 1972:24). The soil is sticky, black clay, making travel impossible for vehicles about six months of the year. During this wet season the Murle gather into large, semipermanent villages on land which is slightly higher than the surrounding flooded areas. Most of the social life takes place during this four-month period when the people are together.

As the land begins to dry up, the men move off with the cattle in search of new grazing. The old people, women, and children remain in the village for a few more months with a few milk cows which graze nearby. By December it is so dry that they are at last forced to abandon the village and go out in search of grazing and water. The clay has become dry and hard, and deep cracks appear in the ground making walking difficult. The Murle have an expression for this time of the year: "the season when the world is hot and ugly" (Lewis 1972:26). Time drags by during this season, and the Murle do their best just to exist until the rains return and bring them water and new grass. It is overall a difficult existence, but one to which the Murle have adapted.

The Highland Murle who live on the Boma plateau have a more moderate climate since the plateau is about five thousand feet high. This plateau is actually the foothills of the Ethiopian mountains which extend into Sudan. The plateau has spectacular cliffs and several immense volcanic plugs standing several thousand feet tall. This region was created by volcanic activity, but has had a great deal of erosion since then, causing the mountains to be rounded and broken. The slopes are rocky, supporting only small trees, but the valley bottoms are extremely fertile. Some of the trees here are ten feet in diameter. Rainfall is about twelve hundred millimeters a year (Barbour 1961:47), and small streams flow most of the time. When they dry up, it is possible to get enough water from springs to maintain human life. The amount of rainfall and the fertile soil makes cultivation easy for the Highland Murle who are able to store enough food to get them through the dry season.

The primary subsistence focus of the Lowland Murle is their cattle which provide both milk and blood to the Murle diet. These cattle are similar to those of the Dinka, and were probably originally stolen from the Dinka when the Murle first moved into the area. The Murle love their cattle so much that when a man dies, he is laid in the cattle kraal so his cows can say goodbye. They have an extensive cow-referent vocabulary, having words for all possible cow colors, sizes, ages, sexes, and horn shapes. These vast herds must be kept on the move, especially during the dry season, to find enough grazing.

During the wet season when the Lowland Murle regroup on higher ground, the women plant fields of millet and corn. Some of this is stored and later carried with them on their dry-season treks when milk is low. Gardening, however, is regarded as of secondary importance to keeping cattle.

The Murle also hunt to supplement their diet. The plains on which they live have vast herds of game such as white-eared kob (*Kobus kob leucotis*), tiang (*Damaliscus korrigum tiang*), and various gazelle. At certain times of year these animals congregate in tremendous herds and migrate to new grazing areas. The Murle call these migrations "the tree of meat" (Lewis 1972:33). During these migrations it is possible for the Murle to kill large numbers, either by spearing them or by dropping objects on them when the herds pass under trees (oral communication, Peter Parr, Feb. 1975). This meat is sun dried and kept for future use; however, since the wild herds are continually moving, they are not a dependable food source.

Murle also eat fish. When the rivers recede at the end of the rains, they leave isolated pools which are heavily populated with fish. Large groups of people go fishing together. First the men thrust at the fish with their spears, then the women follow in a solid line, catching the fish with inverted baskets. These fish are dried, but again they are not a primary food source.

Murle (Beir)

Highland Murle are actually part of the same group, but since they live in a different environment, they have a different lifestyle. The mountains in which they live contain the tsetse fly that infects cattle with sleeping sickness, so it is impossible for them to keep livestock (oral communication, Ahad, Jan. 1975). Their area is well watered since it receives about twelve hundred millimeters of rain per year (Barbour 1961:47). The area is mostly rocks, but the Highland Murle have learned to plant their gardens in valley bottoms where the annual rains carry silt and adequate moisture to grow their crops. Their gardens have more variety and are more fruitful than most others in eastern Sudan. They grow millet and corn as their staple crops, but also cultivate okra, bananas, pineapple, mangoes, coffee, and tobacco.

Although there is a hundred-mile gap between the Lowland and Highland Murle, they do stay in contact with each other. The medicine men for the entire group live in the mountains where they are able to find more plants and herbs for their practices. High quality tobacco and coffee are also grown by the Highland Murle and are traded with the people on the plains (oral communication, Trader, Jan. 1975).

The Lowland Murle build two kinds of houses: temporary shelters when they are herding their cattle, and larger dwellings in the permanent villages. Temporary shelters are hastily constructed of branches and grass and follow no set form. The larger dwellings are located in villages that are usually strung out along a river.

Building houses is predominately women's work, although the men will assist in cutting the larger poles. When a girl is married, she is given an axe by her family so she can build her new house. When completed, these houses look like large haystacks. Sticks are cut and pushed into the ground to form the circumference of the new house. These sticks are bent inwards and tied together at the top, making the framework look like a large inverted basket. Supports are placed in the center to help hold the weight of the roof. Loose sheaves of grass are then tied onto this framework with bark. No intricate thatching or trimming is done, and the thatch reaches all the way to the ground.

All the houses are built with two rooms: a small porch and a living area. The porch is actually part of the entryway into the main room. A floor plan of a Murle house (fig. 24) is presented by Lewis (1972:44).

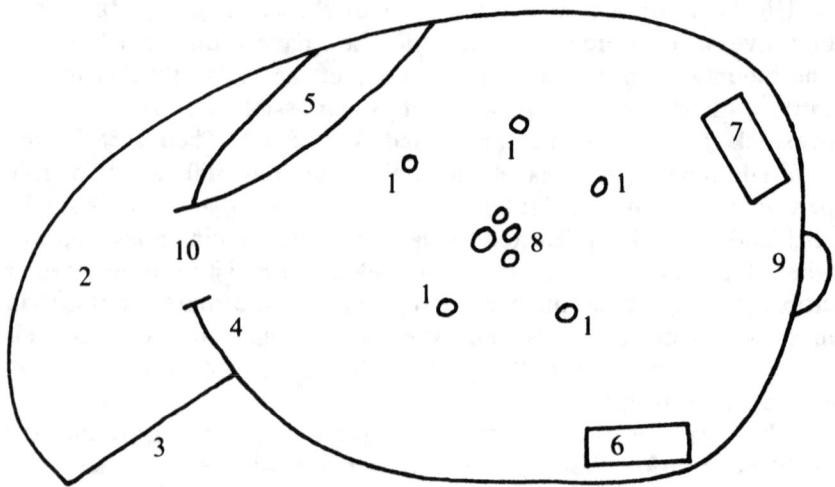

Fig. 24. Floor plan of Murle house

1. Supports
2. Porch
3. Doorway of porch
4. Place for visitors
5. Enclosure for sheep and goats
6. Woman's bed
7. Platform bed (children)
8. Fire
9. Cupboard
10. Room entrance

    The houses of the Lowland Murle are large, often measuring thirty feet in length and ten feet in height. The thick grass thatch keeps them relatively cool during the day, and at night dried cow dung is burned for its sweet smell and to control the mosquitoes.

    The Highland Murle build their houses in a similar style, but these houses are smaller and more rounded; some of them even have a slight peak on the roof. The cooler climate in the hills may be a reason for smaller houses since they are easier to keep warm at night. Highland Murle build small homesteads on hillsides among the rocks. The limited amount of flat ground may also be a reason for building smaller houses. In the center of each homestead is a large circle of stones, often standing three feet high. The people congregate in this circle at night around a fire for talk and companionship.

    Murle history is repeated in the pattern of homestead layout. Each house is placed to represent one of the four stops in the Murle migration.

Murle (Beir)

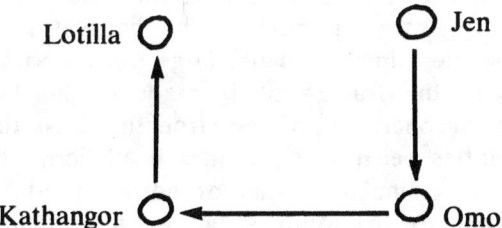

Fig. 25. Murle migration stops

In an ideal Murle family there are four wives, each of whom has her own house. These houses are placed in special positions according to the wife's seniority (see fig. 26). The senior wife takes the position of Jen on the northeast of the compound. This is the most important location since Jen is the source of life, and is the direction from which the rains come. The other wives place their houses in order of seniority (Lewis 1972:41). At the present time, most Murle do not have four wives, so this system is often disregarded; however, to them it is the ideal situation, and they try to conform to it as much as possible.

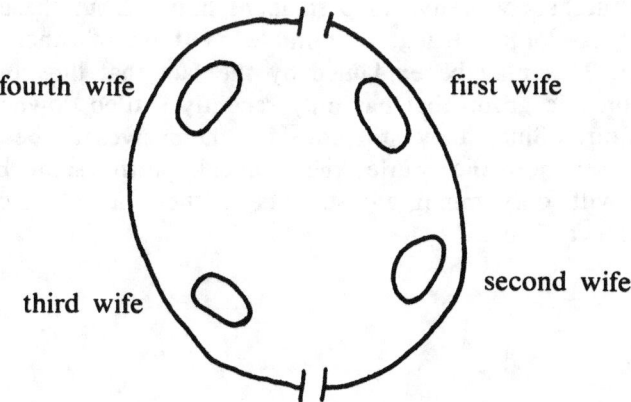

Fig. 26. Position of houses in a Murle homestead

Among the Lowland Murle a fence is sometimes built around the entire homestead so that the cattle may be kept inside at night for protection.

Murle houses are different from any others in Sudan, but are well adapted to their plains environment. The houses have no large superstructure of poles simply because large trees are unavailable in this area. Instead, the framework is made of small sticks tied together into a hemisphere to provide strength. Grass thatch is put on in great quantities because it provides insulation. The shape of the Murle houses is similar to that of houses used by nomadic peoples of Kenya, only the Murle structures are much larger. The Murle may have borrowed this house form years ago when they were nearer Kenya, and then adjusted it to meet their own needs. It is also possible that the two similar shapes evolved separately with each group adjusting its house forms to meet cultural and environmental demands.

Like the Dinka, the Lowland Murle are transhumant because of the environment in which they live. The change in seasons means a change in residence. House forms that are used at any given time reflect the subsistence focus at that time. Larger, more comfortable houses are used when the people live together and are working their fields, while temporary shelters are used in the dry season when the people are following the herds.

The Highland Murle at first seem to be an exception to the initial hypothesis that house form reflects subsistence focus. They are agriculturalists who live in permanent houses, but these structures are not as large, strong, or durable as those of other agricultural groups. This may be explained by the fact that they once were a seminomadic group that has only recently settled down to full-time agriculture. Since they still consider themselves to be part of the larger, seminomadic Murle, they have kept the same basic house forms with only minor adjustments to their new environment and subsistence focus.

Murle (Beir)

MURLE DWELLINGS. Lowland Murle often build their homesteads on open plains.

A SINGLE HOME. Permanent houses are built on higher ground above the flood level and resemble a giant haystack.

HIGHLAND MURLE HOMESTEAD. Each wife has a house of her own.

A HIGHLAND MURLE HOUSE. Highland houses are small, slightly domed, and nearly round except for the entryway extending from one side.

DIDINGA

The Didinga live in southeastern Sudan near the juncture of the Uganda, Kenya, and Sudan borders (see fig. 23). Most of them live in a small mountain range called the Didinga Hills. Their total population is estimated to be about 51,000 (1955 census).

Linguistically, they are in the same family as the Murle, and at one time they probably spoke the same language. They have been isolated from each other for at least a hundred years, and the two languages have changed so much that they are no longer mutually intelligible. Yet they are similar enough that a Murle or a Didinga can still learn the other's language within a very few days.

Some of the Didinga claim that they have always lived in these hills (oral communication, Didinga teacher, Feb. 1975); however, their language shows definite similarities with that of the Murle. They were probably part of the Murle migrations from Ethiopia into Sudan. They then settled in the Didinga Hills which is similar terrain to that which they left in Ethiopia. The origins of the Didinga are still basically conjectural and need to be studied in more detail. In more recent times, the Didinga have been in contact with the British and the Arabs. The British found the climate comfortable in these hills, so they built a town at Nagichot in the 1930s. When the Arabs took over after independence, they moved the administration to Kapoeta since they found Nagichot too cold. During the civil war, the southern troops concentrated in these mountains and some fighting and bombing took place here, but the Anyanya kept control of the mountains until the end of the war.

The Didinga Hills are a range reaching up to about seven thousand feet in elevation and covering about sixteen hundred square miles. There are rocky peaks and deep valleys surrounding a high plateau. The vegetation at the base of the hills is deciduous woodland and tall grass, but in gradually ascending altitudes, this gives way to bamboo and larger trees. The top of the range consists of large montane forests and open fields of grass. Rainfall in the area is usually above a meter (Barbour 1961:47), but occasionally fails, producing severe drought. Temperatures are moderate, reaching about 80° F during the day and dropping to 50° at night.

The Didinga have a mixed agricultural and cattle economy. Their primary subsistence focus is agricultural, so they live in permanent homesteads where each wife has her own garden within walking distance. Gardens are built on steep slopes where farming is done by the slash-and-burn technique. Crops are planted around charred logs, well fertilized by the ashes. The main crop is corn (maize), which is unusual since everywhere else in Sudan it is millet. Corn is allowed to ripen and dry on the stalk. It is then husked and hung on racks until needed. This dry corn is pounded into flour and eaten in the form of a thick mush.

The Didinga do not keep as many cattle as do peoples of the plains around them. As a rule community herds are watched by a number of young men taking turns. Herds are not kept near any one homestead, but are taken where the grazing is best. During the rainy season, herds are kept on the mountains where the rain brings up new grass. When the rains stop, the streams at higher elevations dry up, so the herders gather the cattle together and drive them down into the lower valleys and plains where the larger rivers feed permanent watering holes. The men who herd the cattle live almost exclusively on blood and milk. To bleed the cattle, a small ten-inch bow is used to shoot a small, blocked arrow. This is shot into the jugular vein of a trussed cow, the block on the arrow keeping it from penetrating too far. Up to a quart of blood is caught in a gourd before the hole in the vein is sealed (Driberg 1930:127). This blood is mixed with milk as a means of supplementing their diet.

Hunting is also undertaken by the men. They often hunt alone or in small bands, but in the past the men would gather together for an annual buffalo hunt. A large buffalo herd would be located and their daily habits observed. Eventually the men would choose a location for an ambush, and up to thirty men would wait in a ravine with their spears in readiness. Then the other hunters would show themselves to the herd and would drive the panicked buffaloes down the ravine past the waiting spearmen (Driberg 1930:259-64). It was possible to kill as many as forty buffalo at a time in this fashion.

Didinga

Rhinoceroses live on the plains to the south, and their thick skins are valuable to the Didinga. These rhino are speared, and the skins are cut into beautiful five-foot black whips edged with brass from spent cartridges. Didinga men are very proud of these and can often be seen carrying a whip rather than a spear.

Each extended family builds its own homestead. Many of these are built on mountain peaks or cliff edges, so are extremely difficult to approach. This placement of homesteads helps keep them safe from the attacks by peoples of the plains who are afraid of heights and of the precarious approaches. Homesteads are sometimes surrounded by a heavy wood fence with a gate that can be closed at night to keep out intruders. When flying over the hills, it is intriguing to see some of these homesteads located in the most inaccessible and precarious places. During recent years, since there has been little fighting with the neighboring tribes, many contemporary houses are being built in flat areas, and fences are not always erected around the compound.

The Didinga have basically two kinds of dwellings: temporary shelters erected by cattle herders or by women guarding their gardens, and houses in the permanent homesteads. Temporary shelters are usually made by forming a rough framework of sticks and tying some grass loosely on top. The cattle herders make simple shelters, whereas the women put more time and effort into their garden shelters. The women's shelters provide shade during the heat of the day, and when the crops are ripening it is often necessary for them to stay in the fields to guard against birds, monkeys, and baboons. Stronger walls are then built, and a woman and her children may stay there for several weeks until the crop is harvested.

In the permanent homesteads, each woman has her own house inside the fenced courtyard. These houses are round and from fifteen to thirty feet in diameter (see photo). Heavy posts are driven into the ground and are then joined by walls of interwoven split bamboo which creates a neat, uniform appearance. Mud is packed in the cracks to insulate the house from the cold. The framework for the conical roof is also made of bamboo tied together with bark. Thatch is tied on in layers, giving it a tiered look. The tiered roof is not as accentuated as those among the Toposa, but utilizes basically the same technique. Some of the houses in the new larger villages are now square, but manifest the same construction techniques as the round houses. These square houses probably show the influence of the rectangular brick houses which the British built at Nagichot.

Figure 27 is a basic outline of a small homestead observed near the ruins of Nagichot. It contained five houses inside the heavy fence and two houses outside. A large quantity of dried corn was hanging from several large racks. There was also a sitting area built of raised logs forming an amphitheater around a central fire. Here the people would gather at night to sit and talk.

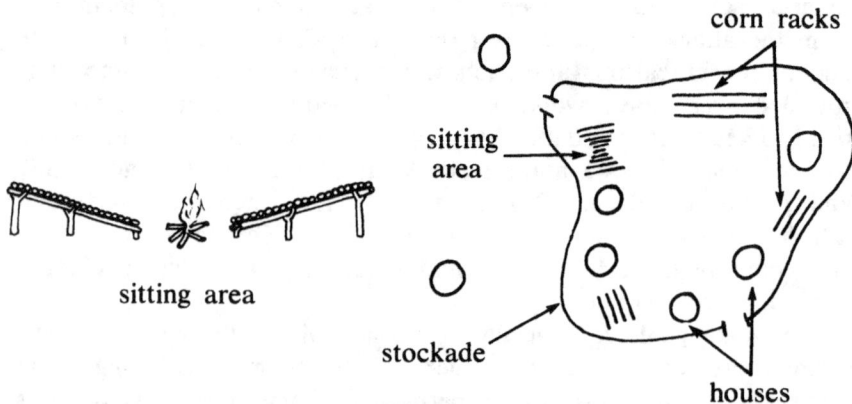

Fig. 27. Didinga homestead

Each homestead is headed by a man who is officially in charge of that homestead. When the head of a homestead dies, he is buried in the courtyard and a cairn of stones is piled on his grave. Then the entire homestead is pulled down and utterly destroyed. Even the pottery is broken, and the sitting stones are rolled away so that no trace exists. A new homestead is then built in a new location (Driberg 1930:170–71). This custom is no longer practiced in the large westernized villages, but among the small homesteads in the mountains, it is still done (oral communication, Didinga headmaster, Feb. 1975).

The large dwellings of the Didinga are a reflection of their subsistence focus. Since these people are primarily agricultural, their houses are situated in semipermanent locations within walking distance of their fields. The Didinga live in these houses all during the year, so considerable time and effort are spent in constructing strong, durable houses which are adequate for all seasons. Hastily constructed shelters are built only under circumstances where they will be used for a short time.

Didinga 69

DRYING CORN. The Didinga tie corn by the husks onto suspended poles to keep it safe and dry until it is needed.

DIDINGA PERMANENT DWELLINGS. Large conical houses are located on a plateau in the Didinga Hills. Smaller buildings are used for storing corn.

WOMEN'S TEMPORARY SHELTERS. Didinga women build temporary shelters in which to rest when working in their fields.

A CONTEMPORARY DIDINGA HOUSE. Many houses near the town of Nagichot are now built with rectangular walls made of interwoven bamboo.

TOPOSA

The Toposa live in the extreme southeastern corner of southern Sudan. Their territory is bordered on the west by the Didinga and Boya Hills, and on the east by the base of the Ethiopian Highlands. Their population numbers about 120,000 (1955 census).

Their linguistic classification is Para-Nilotic, and within this family they are included in the Turkana-Karamajong dialect cluster. This cluster contains six major peoples: Teso, Toposa, Jiye, Karamajong, Dodoth, and Turkana. Their languages are sufficiently similar that a person speaking one dialect is capable of understanding any other, although often with some difficulty.

All of the peoples within this cluster seem to have come from the same area—probably northern Uganda. As the original group expanded, sections of it split off and migrated to other locations, forming the present configuration (Ehret 1968:174). Over the years, the different dialects have evolved separately into their present forms. The Jiye were the first to split off from the main group; they moved north into the present Toposa area. Then about 1800, the Toposa moved to Liyoro in northern Kenya. About 1890, the Turkana appeared and pushed the Toposa out of Liyoro and into Sudan. As the Toposa moved into Sudan they found the Murle in the southern region and forced them north to their present location. The Jiye, being less numerous, were caught between the Toposa and Murle where the environment was hostile to survival. They have not yet settled in a livable location, but are presently beginning to intermarry and live with Toposa. The Dodoth were the last to move, and are presently found in northern Uganda, just north of the Karamajong (Nalder 1937:65–81).

It is obvious in many ways that the Toposa are related to the peoples of northern Kenya and Uganda. The language is the most obvious indicator. Other similarities include the breed of cattle herded, the methods of fighting, the use of wells in the river beds, and the wearing of ostrich egg necklaces.

The environment in which the Toposa live is essentially flat, dry country, with a good deal of acacia thorn bush. River beds are wide and filled with sand. Water runs only after hard rains, so it is usually necessary to dig deep wells in the sand in order to procure water. Along the river beds are gallery forests of tall yellow fever trees. The vegetation and climate are very similar to the semideserts of northern Kenya, and in actuality are the northernmost reaches of this desert.

The Toposa are essentially a pastoral people, but their cattle are of a different breed than those found in the rest of southern Sudan. These cattle are much stockier, having shorter horns and larger humps than those of central Sudan. The group is seminomadic, and during the dry season older people and children are left in the villages while the rest are out with the cattle in temporary camps. While in the cattle camps, their diet is mainly blood and milk. They are the only group of southern Sudan to possess donkeys which are used to carry their belongings when moving from camp to camp. Herds of goats are also kept for their meat.

Millet is also a staple food of the Toposa, fields being located in the vicinity of the villages. Sometimes a number of these fields will be surrounded by a single fence, but each plot is individually owned and worked by the women. The millet stored in raised granaries helps the people survive the long dry season.

Toposa villages are built near a source of water, and a large number of houses are concentrated in a small area. Since most of the acacia trees in this region are short and twisted, and the grass does not grow to great heights as it does in better-watered areas of Sudan, the houses which are built from poles and grass are not as large as houses elsewhere. Their building style is unique among the Sudanese and Kenyans. These one-room houses are built of a framework of sticks covered with grass, but their appearance is more bowl shaped. The thatching continues to ground level. Since the grass is short, it is cut in small bunches and tied into the framework in tiers. There may be as many as twenty tiers to a house, and each of these is neatly edged, giving the house the appearance of a beehive. Thorn bush is often stacked around the houses to keep goats from eating the thatch.

Within this basic style there is some variation. Most of the larger dwellings are built directly on the ground; however, each village has numerous smaller houses built on posts as much as six feet high. Some of these smaller houses are used as granaries and chicken coops, while others are used for sleeping. Regardless of whether the house is raised or on the ground, the thatching pattern is the same. There was no indication of mud ever being used as construction material even though it is available.

Within the villages are separate sitting areas. An area about fifteen feet in diameter is encircled by a heavy wooden fence. A fire is built in the center, and here the people meet at night to talk. The shade under the raised houses is also used as a sitting and resting place during the day.

In addition to the houses, each compound builds a structure for cooking food. This is not thatched, but consists of sticks stacked into a tepee-like shape.

Entire villages are surrounded by thorn-bush fences. This is supposedly to keep out wild animals such as lions, and to prevent attack by other groups. The entrance to each village is through an archway of heavy poles. Many of these fences have been neglected in recent years and are not as impenetrable as they used to be (oral communication, Toposa teacher, Feb. 1975). The cattle are kept in separate fenced kraals outside the village, and some of the men always stay with them for their protection.

These villages and houses are built entirely from the meager materials in the environment around them. From these the Toposa have developed a house form which is not only practical, but also stands out for its beauty and technique. Their house form seems to be a mixture of the hemispherical houses built by the nomadic peoples of Kenya and the conical-roofed houses of Sudan.

The area in which the Toposa live is not affected by yearly flooding. It is therefore not necessary to build on high ground far from a permanent water source. The Toposa are able to build villages near enough to a water supply that they can live there all year long. It is necessary for some of the people, however, to live away from the village in order to provide grazing for the cattle. Again the permanent villages reflect the building of agriculturalists while the temporary cattle camps are the structures of nomads.

A MILLET GRANARY. The Toposa store millet in an elevated, thatched granary. They use a branched stick as a ladder to reach the opening.

TOPOSA SLEEPING HOUSE. Ground-level houses are thatched with grass. Thorn bush branches are piled around the walls to keep the goats from eating the thatch.

Toposa 75

A TOPOSA VILLAGE. Thorny fences surround large villages for protection.

A TOPOSA COOK HOUSE. In contrast to the neat appearance of the dwellings, the kitchen remains a framework tepee of sticks.

LOTUKO

The Lotuko are a large group of peoples living in a fifty-mile radius of Torit. The total population of this group is about 116,000 according to the 1955 census.

Linguistically, they are classified as Para-Nilotic. The Lotuko were once one of the many small groups living in the Torit area, speaking closely related languages. These groups included Logis, Logiri, Lomya, Dongotono, Lowudo, Lorwana, Lopit, Lango, Koriok, and Kokoiya. Each of these considered itself to be separate, with a separate language. When the British administration was set up in Torit, it was decided to make Lotuko the official language of the area. Lotuko, therefore began to be written and was used in the schools. People from neighboring dialects learned Lotuko easily since it was similar to their own languages. Over the years Lotuko has become the general name for all of the peoples within the dialect cluster.

The Lotuko, who seem to have lived in this area a long time, can remember no history of migrations or of having origins in some other area of Africa. Ehret (1968:163) suggests that the ancestral home of all Nilotic and Para-Nilotic peoples was an area along the southern fringe of the Ethiopian highlands near Lake Rudolf. If so, the Lotuko originated quite near their present location. One of the earliest Lotuko groups seems to have lived at Mt. Iliu, northeast of Torit, and from this source smaller groups split off over the years, dispersing to their present locations and developing their own dialects. These small groups usually stayed in their separate areas, but did at times unite to fight the Anuak from the north and the Toposa in the east. When the British made Lotuko the official language, these splinter groups again became one unit. Today most of the people of the Torit area consider themselves to be Lotuko, and speak that language. Only the more remote groups such as Lokoiya, Dongotono, and Lango have attempted to maintain their own dialects and identities.

The Torit area is flat and hot, and is bordered by small rocky hills. The vegetation is generally low-rainfall woodland savannah alternating with plains. There are a number of sandy riverbeds which are usually dry and which are bordered by large numbers of *Borassus* palms. The land to the west and south of Torit is also woodland savannah but has a higher rainfall, so the vegetation is more dense.

The Lotuko are primarily an agricultural group whose diet consists mostly of millet. This is planted in large fields cleared by the men and planted by the women. These fields are often placed at the base of a hill where they get maximum water run-off. Seed-eating birds are a constant threat to the millet, so tall platforms are built in the fields and small boys are assigned to spend their days sitting in these towers, shooting rocks with their slingshots to keep away the birds.

During the late dry season the *Borassus* palms along the riverbeds produce a large, orange fruit. The chewy fibers of this fruit provide the Lotuko with both moisture and nutrition (oral communication, Nikoli Mvuni, Mar. 1975).

Most of the villages have cattle, sheep, and goats. At night these are kept in large kraals within the village stockade. At the end of a grazing day the cattle are led single file through a wooden arch from which hangs a bell. Each cow is counted as it rings the bell with its back and enters the kraal for the night (Seligman 1932:306-7).

The Lotuko do not usually live in the hills, but like to build their villages directly at the base of these rocky outcroppings. These hills are often located far from a permanent water source, but a site near the hills seems more important than a site near the sandy riverbeds. Water is often short during the dry season, and in some areas the women walk as much as eight hours a day to fetch water (oral communication, Nikoli Mvuni, Mar. 1975).

Lotuko villages are unique in that they are so large. Some villages such as Tirongole are reported to contain more than three thousand houses (Seligman 1932:307). Each individual family unit places its houses around a small courtyard, then a thick strong fence of poles is built around the entire compound. In past years these thick fences were extended all around the village and cattle kraals until there were only narrow, twisting paths leading from one house to another. The purpose of these twisting paths was to prevent mass night attacks by enemies. Since the paths were so narrow, it was impossible for a large group of warriors to attack at one time. Also, cattle could only be led out of the village in single file, so the paths also restricted the number of cows lost in a cattle raid. Now with relative peace, these paths have been widened, and there is easier access to the houses and cattle kraals.

Inside the villages are tall platform towers reaching as high as thirty feet which are used for lookouts as well as being associated with age classes and initiation into these classes. When boys enter manhood they are then allowed to sit on these towers, indicating that they have achieved a new class distinction.

Houses are large with tall, peaked roofs, and are among the most elegant looking in all of Sudan. A mud wall is built in a circle about four feet high. A framework of poles tied together with bark is then placed on the walls so the poles almost touch the ground. This framework is thatched with either grass or palm leaves, depending on which is more readily available. Grass thatch is smooth and reaches almost to the ground. A small cap of grass is tied onto the peak to make it completely waterproof. The palm thatch is similar except that it is made from *Borassus* palm fronds laid one over the other, forming a thatch that is rougher looking than the grass, but just as effective in keeping out the rain. The doors into these houses are very low, and one must bend double to enter. This makes it difficult for an enemy to enter a house since it puts him at the homeowner's mercy.

The houses are up to thirty feet tall. The diameter of each being about twenty feet, it is airy and spacious inside. A low wall runs across the center of the house and forms two rooms. On this wall are set large clay water pots.

These tall, stately houses are cool and comfortable as well as fortified against human or animal prowlers. The Lotuko use the available material to build a house which is more than just practical—one that also satisfies a cultural desire for beauty. The primary subsistence focus of the Lotuko is agriculture. The villages are therefore built near the fields; houses are of a permanent nature and are occupied all during the year.

Lotuko

VILLAGE ON A TERRACED HILLSIDE. Some Lotuko crowd their houses together on terraced hillsides for security.

A PLATFORM TOWER IN A LOTUKO VILLAGE. Besides the stockade around the houses, protection is gained by the use of a lookout tower.

LOTUKO HOUSE UNDER CONSTRUCTION. Tall, graceful houses have a low, inner mud wall over which is woven a framework of sticks. Grass or palm fronds provide a smooth thatch covering.

LONGARIM (BOYA)

The Longarim live at the base of the Boya Hills which are the most northern hills connected to the Didinga range. They are often called Boya by their neighbors after the area in which they live. The population of this group is about eight thousand although all of them were not included in the recent census.

They are linguistically classified as among the Didinga-Murle group. The Didinga consider the Longarim to be their backward brothers and include them in the Didinga tribe. The Longarim resent this and claim they are a totally independent group from the Didinga; however, linguistic data show that they are very close and have similar origins.

The history of the Longarim is tied in closely with that of the Murle and Didinga. They were probably all once part of the same migration into Sudan from Ethiopia. Lewis (1972:54) thinks that the Longarim were originally the fourth political clan of the Murle. He states that the Longarim had a quarrel with the other Murle clans and moved south to the Boya Hills about three generations ago. Although the Longarim have had enough contact with the Murle and Didinga to keep their language similar, there have been some cultural changes. Since they are near to the Toposa on the east and the Lotuko on the west, there have been borrowings from both.

The Boya Hills are a granite spur running north from the Didinga Hills. At the base of the hills the land is flat and covered with a mixture of acacia species. Between the trees the ground is bare with little of the tall grass which characterizes much of Sudan. There are sandy riverbeds through the area which are normally dry; nevertheless, water can be obtained by digging wells in the sand. Along the rivers are *Borassus* palms whose fruit is eaten by the Longarim. Rainfall is not heavy, and most of the needed water comes down the rivers from the mountains to the south. Temperatures are hot, between 90° and 100° F, but low average humidity makes the climate more comfortable than the western Sudan.

The Longarim people dress in a fashion similar to the Toposa, have the same hair styles, and use the same weapons. They have small herds of cattle and goats, both of the same varieties as the Toposa. There is an overlap with Toposa boundaries, so that groups are becoming mixed. Young men take the cattle away to graze, leaving only a few near the permanent villages. At the present time the Longarim are primarily agricultural. Since the region is dry, the only crop that does well is millet, so this is the staple food.

In the past, the Longarim were well known for their fighting prowess. Men made frequent raids on neighbors, stealing cattle, food, and women. The Longarim never spent much time caring for their own herds or cultivating their own gardens since they could always go on a raid to meet their needs. In recent times this raiding has been prohibited by the government, resulting in more emphasis on cultivation (oral communication, Chief Joseph Wapuwa, Mar. 1975).

Longarim villages are located near rocky hills, but houses are not built on the hills since the Longarim prefer sites directly at the base of the rocks. Anywhere from four to twenty-five houses are located in a tightly concentrated village, and a large thorn fence is built around the perimeter of the whole village. There is one main entrance through this thorn stockade—a long archway made of heavy poles. The fence and archway were originally built to keep out attackers since many of the peoples whom the Longarim raided attempted to retaliate in vengeance (oral communication, Chief Joseph Wapuwa, Mar. 1975). The archway permits no more than one man to enter the village at a time, thus preventing a mass attack. Within the stockade are not only the houses and courtyards of the people, but also various kraals for the goats and cows.

The houses themselves are usually cylindrical with tall, conical roofs. The walls are of wattle and daub. The framework for the roof rests on these walls and is carefully thatched. To thatch their roofs, the Longarim tie grass into small bundles about two inches thick resembling grass brooms. These are then tied side by side to the framework, starting with the eaves and proceeding up to the peak. The caps of the roofs are often made of fronds from the *Borassus* palms. Granaries and chicken houses are built on raised platforms with walls woven of small sticks and roofs thatched with palm fronds.

If the Longarim did move from the Murle area several generations ago, they have made a great adjustment in house form from the Murle style to their present form. This change may have come about for several reasons. The new environment into which they moved has a larger variety of building materials, making possible house styles involving longer, heavier poles. Living in a hostile area and being forced to defend themselves caused them to group together in tightly packed villages and to fortify themselves with thorn fences and arched gateways. Their house form seems to be a combination of styles borrowed from the peoples around them: the walls are similar to the Didinga, the tiered thatching and archways to the Toposa, and the tall roofs to the Lotuko. In traveling around on their raids, the Longarim may have observed the houses of these various peoples, and in building their own dwellings have adopted some of the things that were practical for their own situation, but now a house form has evolved that is uniquely Longarim.

CYLINDRICAL HOUSES. An inner low wall of wattle and daub is covered by a tall, cylindrical roof of woven sticks. Short bundles of grass are used for thatching.

A FENCED VILLAGE. The Longarim use thorny fences both for protection and for privacy.

IK (TEUSO)

The Ik are referred to as Teuso in the older books on Sudan, but little was known of them except their name. They are located south of the Didinga in the southeastern mountains of Sudan, their territory extending into the Kidepo Valley and mountains of northeastern Uganda. They have always been a small group, probably numbering under three thousand, but exact figures are unavailable.

Tucker recently spent some time analyzing their language in Uganda. The language has a great many implosive and explosive sounds and shows little similarity to any of the other languages in east or central Africa. Tucker claims that the nearest language he could find was classical Middle Kingdom Egyptian (Turnbull 1972: 42). This leads to interesting theories on their origins. Sutton (1968: 84) places them in the Nyangiya group, but this group has not yet been classified, and more study needs to be done. The name Ik is the name these people call themselves. Turnbull studied the Ik in Uganda for several years. His book, *The Mountain People* (1972), is the source for most of the information in this section, since he is the only person that has ever studied them for any length of time.

The mountains in which the Ik live are for the most part dry and rocky and unsuitable for agriculture, but there are high valleys containing permanent water and hardy trees. The mountains in Sudan contain more vegetation because of a higher rainfall, but the more southern mountains in Uganda are dry and contain mostly scrub acacia. The Kidepo Valley running between the two mountain ranges is flat and low, containing open acacia bush with adequate water, grass, and foliage along the river. This valley has large herds of elephant and buffalo as well as many species of antelope. During the rains the valley gets flooded and the black clay becomes sticky. Animals move up into the mountains until the valley dries out.

The Ik were originally hunters and gatherers who wandered the mountains and valleys in search of food. They were considered excellent hunters by the Didinga and were feared for their witchcraft. They seem to be the original inhabitants of this area, with the Didinga and Dodoth moving in later. The Didinga considered the Ik an ancient race and respected their intricate knowledge of the mountains (Driberg 1930:290–91). Although they spent much of the year in the mountains, their favorite hunting area was the Kidepo Valley in northern Uganda. The Ik migrated in regular cycles from the mountains to the valley and back again, depending on the rains and game movement. Ik territory was later divided by the new colonial powers among three countries: Sudan, Uganda, and Kenya. Just before World War II, the Ik were all encouraged to live in Uganda because the borders took on a new significance as separators of political territories, and the governments did not want the Ik constantly moving between countries. Most of the Ik did move into Uganda, although scattered bands still exist in Sudan and Kenya. Then in the 1960s the Kidepo Valley was made into a national game park. The Ik were removed from this new park and forbidden to hunt there. They were relocated in the dry mountains southeast of the Kidepo Valley where there was little game to hunt. The government encouraged them to turn to agriculture; but their new location was poor agricultural land and, besides, the Ik had no desire to stop hunting and to work in the fields. They planted hastily in ill-prepared fields. Because of low rainfall most of these gardens failed to produce, so famine set in. This was the situation Turnbull found when he arrived in Uganda to study the Ik.

Originally, before government interference, the Ik were able to survive because they were constantly on the move. They traveled in bands, sometimes large and sometimes small, depending on the nature of the area and the food sources available. There was cooperation within these bands with everyone—men, women, and children—participating in the food-gathering process. In the Kidepo Valley these bands would number up to a hundred people since large numbers were needed for hunting. Poles were stuck in the ground, and up to a half mile of nets were suspended between these poles. The women and children would act as beaters to drive the game into the nets where they were speared by the men. Nets were also set up in front of grass fires, entrapping the panicked animals as they fled the flames. The surplus meat from these net hunts was dried and carried with them as emergency provisions. These net hunts involving large groups of people took place infrequently; most of the time the Ik functioned in smaller bands. The men stalked and killed small game with their spears or bows and arrows while the women went out and gathered wild fruit, roots, nuts, and berries. Food was generally scarce and would not support a large or constant population, so the people kept spread out and moving. During certain seasons of the year the Ik would break into even smaller groups and go to special, known locations where they could find termites and wild honey. Their knowledge of their environment and of what was edible helped them exist in a land with little food.

Their original houses were built by making a small igloo-shaped framework of sticks and covering it with grass. These were easy to build and could be put up quickly by the women. Whether a band was staying in an area for three days or three months, the house structures were basically the same. The houses were laid out in no particular order, but friends and relatives would often build their houses close together. Since the Ik existence depended on mobility, not much emphasis was put on their houses other than to offer shelter.

When the Ik were settled in the southern mountains by the government, their way of life changed drastically. They were no longer free to wander and hunt, but were forced into agriculture which they did not like. The starvation which soon faced them completely broke down the old social order. No longer did people cooperate and assist each other, but every person cared only for himself. The demand for food became so great that when something was found to eat, it was not shared, but eaten privately. Turnbull recites many instances of people gorging themselves while their families were literally dying of hunger. Children suffered the most since they were thrown out to fend for themselves as soon as they were weaned. The people continued to live near each other because they needed human contact, but they ceased helping or sharing with each other. This breakdown of their entire culture was reflected in their houses and village construction.

When the Ik were first moved to the southern mountains, they built large permanent villages. They stopped building the hemispherical houses and adopted the house style of the Karamajong to their south. These houses were much larger than the original houses they had abandoned and were more practical as a permanent residence.

The house walls were cylindrical and built of poles stuck in the ground, interwoven with smaller sticks. The conical frame of the roof was made of poles and was well secured to the walls so the roof would not blow off. This frame was then thatched with grass in a tiered style. Although the Ik had copied the Karamajong house style, they did not put as much time into their work. Usually the minimal amount of work was done, and the houses looked untidy in comparison with the carefully built Karamajong houses. This careless workmanship usually resulted in the houses lasting only about three years before they started falling apart. Ik houses were often built on a steep slope with the door of the house always facing downhill so that when it rained, the water would run past the house rather than into it. Inside all the houses a low sleeping platform was built of mud and covered with skins to be used as a bed. These sleeping platforms were always built level even though the houses were on a slope.

Fig. 28. Ik dwelling built on a slope

The village system itself changed drastically under the new social conditions. People still lived close together as they had in the past, but tall fences of wood separated the houses from each other. Each house was in a private, fenced compound containing the house, a granary (usually empty), and a kitchen which was seldom used. A man and his wife would live in a single house, but their children would sleep outside under the granary. A gate called an *asak* was the only way out of the fenced compound leading to an outer courtyard. These gates were extremely low and narrow, making it necessary to crawl in order to get through them. The Ik claimed this was for defense since a man coming through the *asak* on his hands and knees was at the mercy of the man defending his compound. Around all the private compounds was a shared courtyard surrounded by another stockade going around the whole village. Various small gates called *odok* were used to enter the village from the outside.

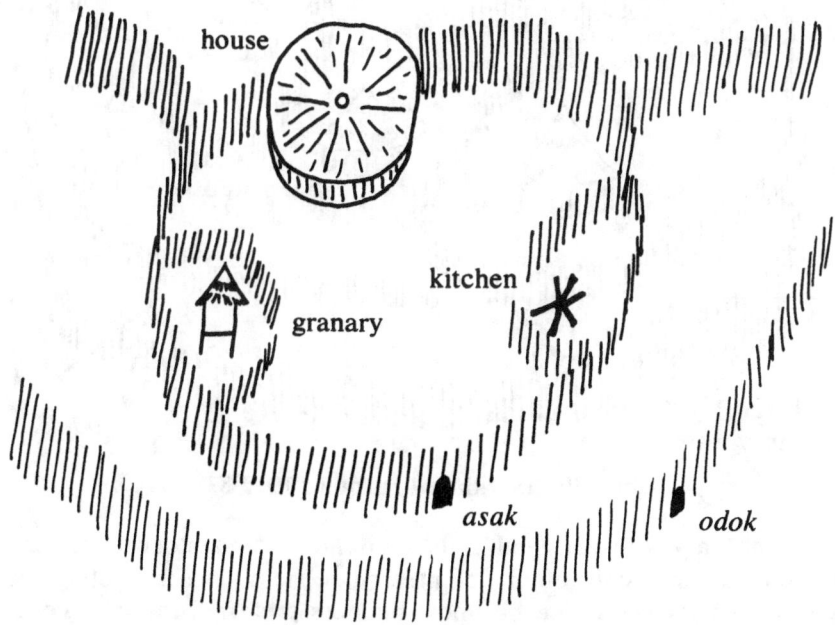

Fig. 29. Private compound (Turnbull 1972:120)

These villages were built with the priority on privacy. All entrances faced outward from the center of the village, and there were no entrances between private compounds. Each compound had its *asak* leading to the outer courtyard and then an *odok* leading out of the village. A person could therefore enter or leave his home without being seen. When food was found, a person could bring it home and hide it without being forced to share it. Even in a large village, the houses in the center had private corridors which allowed them access into and out of the village.

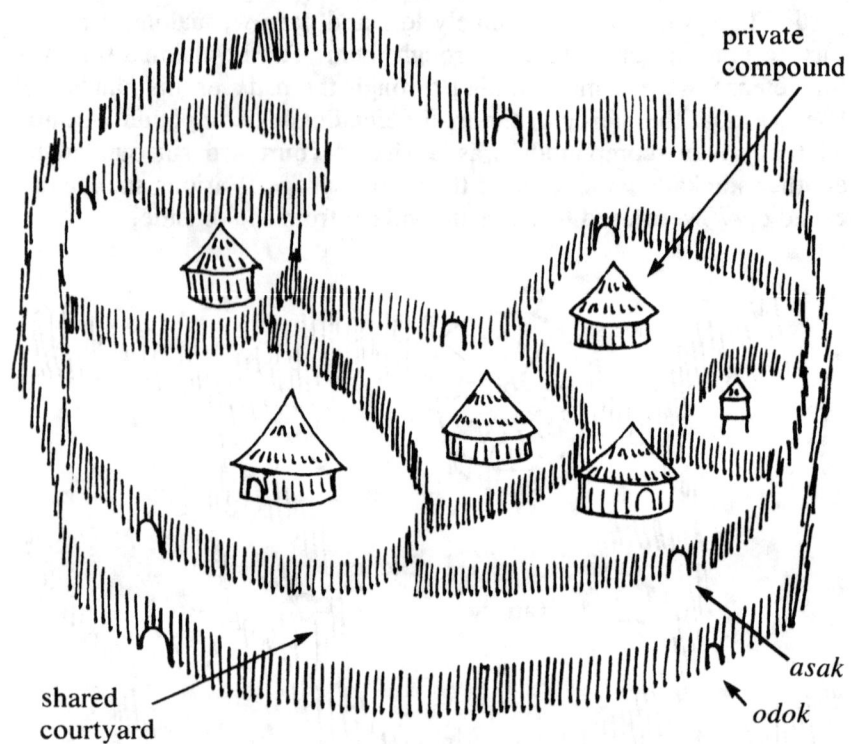

Fig. 30. Ik village (Turnbull 1972:83)

Each family usually built its own house and stockaded compound. Other people often volunteered to help since this obligated the builder to feed them, but most builders preferred to build alone. The outside stockade around the entire village was a shared enterprise, and everyone participated in its construction since it was for the benefit of all. The daily living space was not in the village but was usually a flat place at the edge of a nearby cliff. Here the men would sit all day, seldom speaking, before returning to their private compounds for the night.

Turnbull mentions an unusual incident in his book (1972:210–12). An old lady whose husband had died of starvation became so frustrated with the living conditions that she tore down her house and stockade and left for Sudan. Here she joined with others of her

Ik (Teuso)

family and built a small village in the Sudan mountains. Turnbull followed and found them living in a beautiful, lush valley, surrounded by running streams, and with an abundance of food. The new village had a thin, thorn fence around the perimeter, but there were no private compounds inside. The houses were igloo shaped, and the doors all faced inward to a central courtyard. Here they cooked together and shared their food. It was a happy village with people talking and laughing about the day's events. A few weeks later they left their pleasant village and moved south again to be with the rest of their people. Here they quickly reverted to their selfish and solitary existence.

The original hemispherical houses of the Ik met their needs in their nomadic existence. When they were forced to change their lifestyle, their social behavior also changed. Their new house forms and village structures were direct indications of this social change. They still remember the old ways, and when some temporarily went back to a nomadic existence, they used the original house forms. The most important factor in their change of house forms was not their environment, but the change in their way of life. When their subsistence focus was hunting and gathering it necessitated mobility. This resulted in small, easily constructed houses. Upon becoming agricultural, they immediately abandoned this house form and adopted the larger, more permanent houses of the peoples around them.

PART IV

NORTHERN KENYA

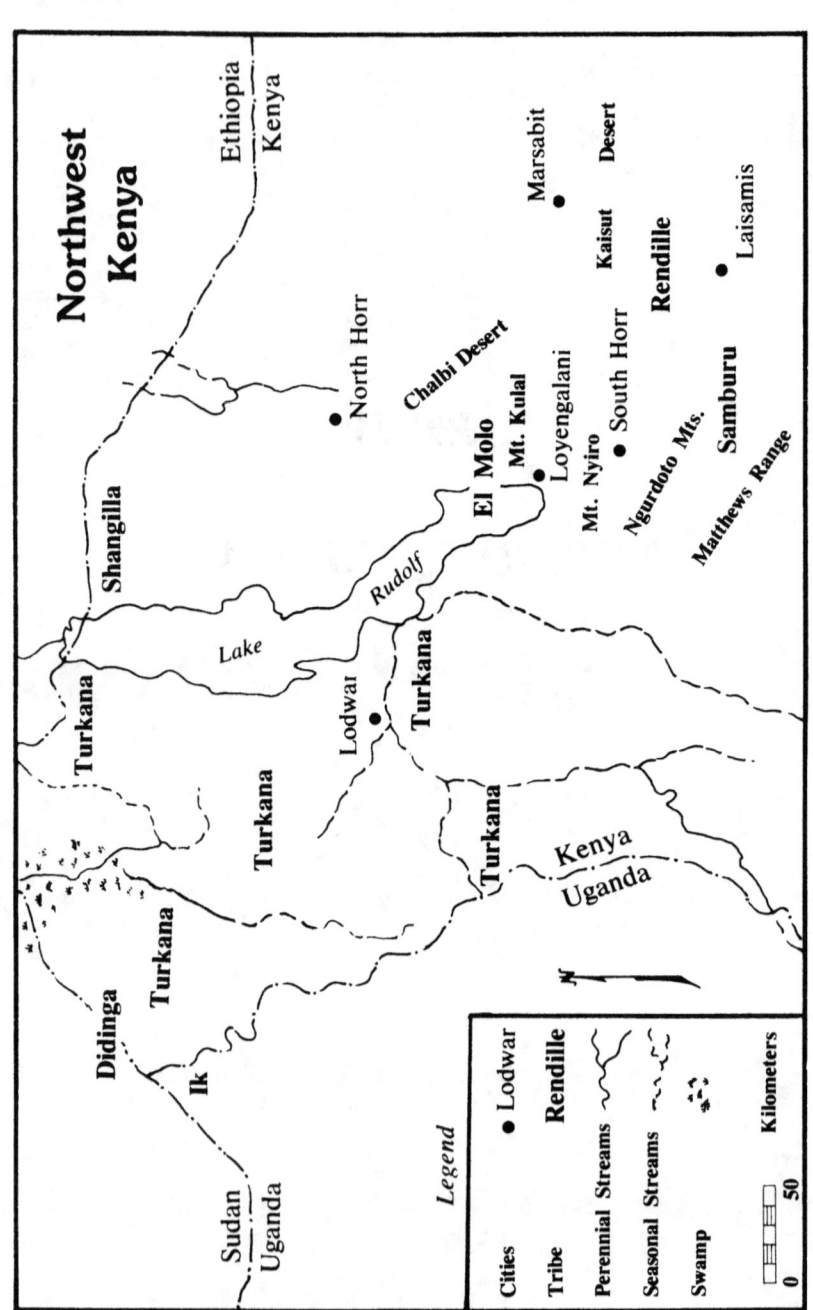

Fig. 31. Northwest Kenya

INTRODUCTION

Most of northern Kenya can be classified as desert or semidesert since it receives less than ten inches of rain per year. Within this large desert is a variety of land forms. The area around Lake Rudolf is volcanic, the terrain consisting entirely of pieces of lava. The Chalbi Desert is white alkali flats, and the Kaisut Desert is primarily sand. At intervals there are old volcanic mountains, some of which reach nine thousand feet in elevation.

Vegetation in the deserts varies from area to area depending on the terrain. In some places it is sparse or nonexistent, although hardy acacia bushes do survive in most areas. Around the infrequent water holes are *dom* palms and larger acacia trees. The tops of the few mountains are better watered and contain thick montane forests. There is a high plateau about sixty miles south of Lake Rudolf which is grass covered, with trees along the watercourses.

Temperatures in northern Kenya can be extreme. In some deserts it can reach 120° F during the day, and since the air is very clear and dry, the temperature drops rapidly at night. This heat fluctuation causes sharp pressure gradients that create tremendous winds. These winds can blow up suddenly several times a day, sometimes carrying a great deal of sand and dust, reducing visibility to near zero. Even though the winds are hot, they bring a semblance of cooling and drive away the bothersome insects.

Lake Rudolf (now Lake Turkana) is a low-lying lake 1,230 feet above sea level (Gulliver 1970:20). It is 170 miles long, running north and south through a volcanic desert. In most areas bordering the lake there is no vegetation whatsoever, just large jagged stones running right to the water's edge. Along the eastern shore there is a small shelf containing grass and hardy desert plants where wild game come to feed. Winds blow off the desert daily and whip the lake into gigantic waves. It is an alkaline lake with no outlet. It is thought to have once been connected to the Nile system, but volcanic uplift left it isolated. The Omo River feeds into it from Ethiopia, and at the south end it is fed by flash floods which infrequently fill the dry watercourses. The lake stays about the same depth from year to year due to evaporation off its surface, but as the years go by the lake becomes more and more alkaline. This alkali supports myriads of salt-tolerant microscopic organisms and algae. Tilapia, which feed on the algae, thrive, and these in turn are eaten by Nile perch which occasionally weigh up to three hundred pounds. Lake Rudolf is reputed to have more fish per cubic yard of water than any other lake in the world. The lake also has one of the largest concentrations of crocodiles left in Africa, and they feed on the larger fish. These crocodiles have not been extensively hunted as in other parts of Africa since the alkaline water makes their skins tough and unsuitable for leather.

"The north and northeast (of Kenya) is one of the most sparsely populated parts of Subsaharan Africa" (de Blij 1964:249). A number of peoples, however, do live in this desert area and along the lake, all of whom have had to make adaptations to the difficult climate in which they live. The specific terrain of each people will be explored further below (see map, fig. 31 for location of the peoples under discussion).

TURKANA

The Turkana are a numerous people living in northwest Kenya. They inhabit all of the area between Uganda and Lake Rudolf and extending south to Pokot country, about twenty-four thousand square miles (Gulliver 1970:42). Their present population is at least eighty thousand and may be much higher.

Linguistically, they are part of the Para-Nilotic family and belong to the Turkana-Karamajong dialect cluster. There have been recent attempts to reduce their language to writing, but in a personal interview with Tucker in London (Oct. 1974), he stated that the sounds are so indefinite that it has been difficult to decide on specific phonetic symbols.

The Turkana live in a harsh environment that is mainly desert and steppe with a *reg* surface. Temperatures remain between 75° and 100° F night and day, and rainfall varies between five and twelve inches a year (Gulliver 1968:56). Vegetation consists mostly of desert scrub with a few trees by the dry, sandy riverbeds. Agriculture is almost impossible, and the area is even inhospitable to livestock since feed is scarce.

The Turkana split off from the Karamajong as a result of a major schism. They moved west and descended the Rift Valley escarpment into their present territory about two hundred years ago (Gulliver 1955:5). This region was so adverse to human existence that the Turkana survived mainly by raiding neighbors and stealing cattle, food, and women. They put increasing pressure on the Samburu, Masai, and Pokot to the south, and eventually might have conquered this more hospitable territory. In 1903 the British made their first contact with the Turkana. Frequent battles took place between the

British and Turkana before the latter were brought under control and a civil administration established in 1926. "The area was one of the last to come under British control in East Africa," says Gulliver (1970:7). With the failure of the rains in the 1950s famine quickly set in, and many Turkana died, even though the British opened famine relief camps on Lake Rudolf. Here Turkana were gathered in large groups and fed by the government. Permanent villages were established, and the people were taught to fish. At the present time many Turkana still live along the lake, but about forty thousand of them have moved south into the high plateau around Maralal and are again infringing on the Samburu grazing areas. Most of the Turkana remain unchanged and still follow their traditional lifestyle.

"The Turkana . . . are nomadic herdspeople with practically no agriculture who depend almost entirely on their animals for subsistence" (Gulliver 1955:2). They are considered by many to be the most nomadic people of Kenya. This constant moving is a direct result of the harsh environment in which they live. The livestock of the Turkana consists of cattle, camels, and goats. Cattle need grazing, so it is necessary to move them from the dry plains to the higher mountains and back again depending on the rains. Turkana dislike the cooler mountains and go there only when it is absolutely necessary for the survival of their cattle. Camels and goats are browsers and better able to exist in the drier areas. If the rains have been good, they are able to survive in the desert year round.

According to Gulliver (1955:11), "In Turkanaland the mode of residence and the nature of all social activities are strongly affected by nomadism." The shelters of the Turkana on trek are extremely simple. During the dry season they merely bend a few branches over and tie them together to supply shade from the sun. During the rainy season a few skins or some grass are thrown over the branches. There are no walls, and therefore no real privacy. No special placement is followed, but everyone just builds his shelter under a convenient bush. These shelters are small and can hold only two or three people. People sleep on the sand after digging a small depression for the hips.

It is necessary on the yearly treks to make about five to ten extended stops. New homesteads are built at each of these stops, and as a result, no homestead is ever permanent but is used for only a few weeks before the people move on. A homestead consists of an extended family. An outer circular fence is made of heaped thorn bushes, the height depending on the danger from predatory animals

Turkana

in that particular area. The main entrance always faces east. Inside the kraal are the wives' houses. Plural wives are frequent among the Turkana, and each wife has two houses—a day house and a night house. The day house, *ekal*, is semicircular and about seven feet high. To supply maximum shade, leafy foliage piled on the roof is frequently added to because the leaves shrivel up. Close by is the wife's night house, *akai*. This is a small dome of bent saplings tied together. The framework is left open during the dry season and covered with skins during the rains. Positioning of houses is important: the senior wife always places her houses to the right of the main entrance to the kraal. Small kraals for the livestock are placed both in the center of the homestead and around the edge.

A homestead with the head of the family and all the wives present rarely exists except during the rainy season when there is enough food for all of the livestock. More often the homesteads are divided, with part of the family taking care of the camels and goats, and others the cattle. The homestead in which the head of the family

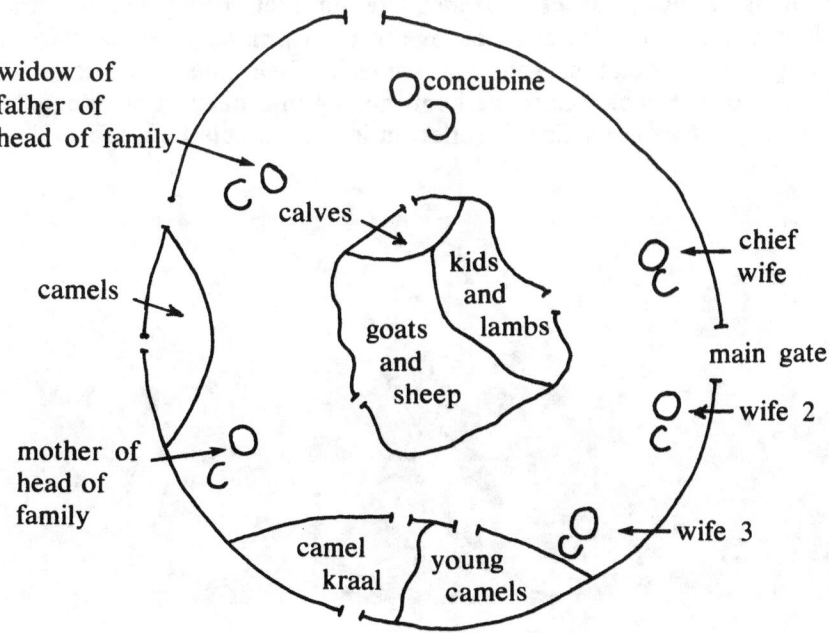

Fig. 32. Turkana homestead (Gulliver 1968:66)

C — a day house   O — a night house

lives is considered the chief homestead and usually remains in the plains. Homesteads are built the same regardless of who inhabits them, and are all called *awi*. There are no distinctions between main homesteads and cattle camps as there are among seminomadic peoples.

The Turkana who have been settled in more permanent villages have begun to build larger, better-constructed houses. The environment still offers limited building materials, but they build a strong igloo-shaped frame of small sticks. *Dom* palm fronds are tied together in long, ten-foot bundles and tied onto the frame so they run from the top of the house to the ground. The thick thatch keeps the interior cool and helps make the house strong enough to resist the frequent winds. Extended families will build their houses around a central courtyard with a palm frond fence around the perimeter, but some houses stand by themselves.

Turkana house forms are shaped by their lifestyle and by the harsh environment in which they live. Their mobile society restricts the amount of time and effort which can be devoted to house building. Simple houses are adequate for their needs because the climate is never cold, and houses are used primarily as shade from the sun and protection from wild animals. Their subsistence focus is their livestock which must be kept moving in order to find adequate pasturage. This nomadism is reflected in their simple house forms.

TURKANA HOMES. These houses are covered with bundles of palm fronds tied to the framework and reaching from the ground to the top of the hemisphere.

A TURKANA SETTLEMENT. Semipermanent Turkana houses are sometimes placed around a fenced courtyard.

A HIGH-DOMED DWELLING. This house has a higher dome than most, but it is made of essentially the same materials as other Turkana houses.

TEMPORARY SLEEPING QUARTERS. During the rainy season, such elevated structures provide protection at night from most of the mosquitoes.

SHANGILLA OF KENYA

The Shangilla are known by many names. Shangilla is the official government name in Kenya; however, they call themselves Dasanech. The Turkana call them Merille and the Borana call them Gallaba. All four of these names occur in the literature, all referring to the same people. The Shangilla are located at the northern tip of Lake Rudolf in Ethiopia and extend down to Iluret, a police post in Kenya on the northeast side of the lake (see fig. 31). The total population is about ten thousand, the majority of whom live in Ethiopia in the Omo River delta. Only a few hundred regularly live inside the Kenya border.

Their linguistic classification is difficult since the languages of this area have not yet been studied extensively and only a few word lists have been procured. The Shangilla can tentatively be classified as among the Gallaba-Arbore group. Few of them are bilingual because they are isolated and have little contact with languages other than Arbore.

At present their history is unknown, although it is likely they moved south to their present location from the Ethiopian mountains. Historical research is currently being carried out at Iluret, so some light should soon be shed on the question.

The Shangilla in Kenya live on low sand hills overlooking Lake Rudolf. The terrain in which they live is sandy desert with only a few hardy plants managing to exist. On the few hundred yards where low vegetation exists near the lake shore, the Shangilla graze their few sheep. The rainfall is low and temperatures high, so agriculture is impossible. However, the Shangilla area in Ethiopia is better watered, and the people there are able to grow millet, so this they trade with the Shangilla in the Kenya desert.

The Shangilla are fierce warriors who traditionally must kill a man before they can be married. Originally they fought with spears and bows and arrows, but now most of them use guns. They go on long, extensive raids looking for victims, and in Kenya no other peoples live within a hundred miles of them. In Ethiopia the Shangilla own war canoes which they sometimes take 150 miles down Lake Rudolf to attack fishing peoples (oral communication, Teasdale, May 1975).

The food of the Kenyan Shangilla consists almost entirely of fish. These are speared by the men who wade out in the shallows of the lake when the tilapia come in to feed along the shore (oral communication, Wilson, May 1975). A few short-haired sheep are also kept which are grazed along the lakeshore until they are killed for their meat and skins. The Ethiopian group are semiagricultural and grow millet which they trade with the Kenyan Shangilla for dried fish. They also have cattle which must be kept on the move to find enough feed.

Shangilla are basically nomadic, and their houses are indications of this lifestyle. Encampments are laid out in a haphazard fashion with no central courtyard. Houses are igloo shaped, about six feet high and fifteen feet in diameter. The terrain has few large trees and very little grass to be used as construction materials. The framework of the house is made by pushing sticks into the ground to form a circle. Then the sticks are bent until they meet in the center at the top, and the ends are tied together.

On top of this light framework is tied skins, mats made of short grass, and anything else such as tin, burlap, and canvas found lying around near the police post. Often desert vines are thrown on top to provide more insulation from the sun. Houses are well braced and strong, but are not entirely rainproof. When occasional rain does soak the houses, the women take them apart, dry the pieces in the sun, and then put them back together again.

Due to the Shangilla preoccupation with basic survival and fighting, they have little time to spend on their houses. Their houses, therefore, are hastily built and can be quickly taken down and the essential parts moved to the next location. Shangilla have built a practical shelter from the meager environment in which they live, and since construction materials are few, much of the house is portable and can be used over and over. Little information has been located regarding the homes of the Shangilla in Ethiopia except that their houses are of a more permanent nature since they practice some agriculture.

HOUSES OVERLOOKING LAKE RUDOLPH. Shangilla houses reflect the harsh environment and nomadic lifestyle. These are located on a sandy hill near the lake.

SHANGILLA HOUSE FRAME. The framework of this house is made of small sticks stuck into the sand in a circle and tied together at the top.

ROOFING MATERIAL. Goatskins and other things are used to cover the framework. These are tied onto it with rope.

EL MOLO

The El Molo are located on two small islands in Lake Rudolf. These islands are in the southeastern part of the lake just north of Loyengalani. The El Molo, the smallest group of Kenya, has a population of about a hundred, which has remained stable at least ninety years. Some writers feel that the people have a secret way of maintaining their population because the islands cannot sustain a larger number. A simpler explanation is that some people leave the islands and intermarry with neighboring groups, taking on a new identity. In recent years some El Molo have moved onto the mainland near Loyengalani where their children can go to the Catholic school.

There has been a great deal of debate about the El Molo origins and linguistic classification. For many years they were thought to be the remnants of the first people who inhabited Kenya, and this has not yet been disproven. A comparison of El Molo word lists with Rendille reveals the languages show some affinity but are not close. El Molo and Shangilla also show some affinity, but all other neighboring languages show no similarities at all. At the present time their language classification is Cushitic, but whether they fall into the Somali or Gallaba family has not yet been determined.

As to origins, an El Molo elder told me that they were originally a part of the Rendille. At one time the whole east side of the lake was inhabited by the Rendille. The elder claimed that those living near the lake learned to fish. Then when the Turkana arrived from the west, they forced the Rendille away from the lake and out into the Kaisut Desert. A small remnant of Rendille became isolated from the main tribe and retreated to the small islands. Over the years through isolation and living a different lifestyle, their language changed enough to no longer be recognizable as Rendille. This story does have merit since it fits into the linguistic data which shows Rendille to be the language most closely related to El Molo, but again, more research needs to be done.

The two small islands on which the El Molo live are only a few hundred yards offshore, and the water between the islands and mainland is shallow. The El Molo, having little fear of the crocodiles, can easily wade ashore. These islands are only about a hundred yards in diameter. They are devoid of any vegetation and are merely low-lying piles of rocks. There is no shade from the hot sun, nor anything to give relief from the strong winds.

The El Molo, in spite of living in such a hostile environment, have managed to eke out an existence for themselves by fishing. The men have some narrow canoes and small rafts made from *dom* palm logs. These are too small to sit in, so the men stand up in them and pole them out to where the fish are. At certain times of day the tilapia come near the shore in large schools looking for food; these are then speared by the waiting men. In some shallows, men merely wade in and stand in the water waiting for fish. It is not unusual to see crocodiles only a few yards away from the fishermen also waiting for the fish to come in and feed. Occasionally nets are used. These are taken out in a canoe and set in a horseshoe shape with both ends touching the shore. Both ends are then pulled in simultaneously bringing in the fish within the reaches of the net. The fishing methods are primitive and not a great deal of time is spent fishing, but they are successful because of the abundance of fish in the lake around them. Their diet consists entirely of fish, and because of this restricted diet there are many signs of vitamin deficiency. Fish is not normally dried since there are always ample quantities of fresh fish available.

Their houses are very simple. Since there is nothing on the islands to provide shelter of any kind, the El Molo go over to the mainland and cut light sticks. These are stuck into the ground in a circle and tied together on top making a hemispherical frame. *Dom* palm fronds are brought from the mainland, then stripped apart, tied in bunches, and tied loosely over the entire frame. The finished result looks like a haystack about five feet high and ten feet in diameter. Houses are not laid out in any special order, but are placed anywhere on the higher ground of the island. There is no central courtyard and no fences, and the doors face in any direction

El Molo

the builders choose. These houses do not keep rain out well since the construction is loose, so it is necessary after a rare rain to take them apart, dry out the fronds, and rebuild the house. The one and only El Molo village is located on bare gravel, and so all building materials must be brought from the mainland.

These houses are simply practical shelters to provide relief from the sun and wind. The limited construction material in the El Molo environment is an important factor in their house form since it sets limitations on what they are able to build. Hemispherical houses stand up well to the strong winds because there are no corners or eaves for the wind to catch. The El Molo have done the best possible with the very few resources at their disposal and have met their basic demands for shelter.

The hypothesis that houses reflect the subsistence focus at first does not seem to apply here. It would seem that since the El Molo are fishermen who live in a permanent location, they would build larger, more permanent homes. In this case, however, the extreme limitation of construction materials available makes the building of larger houses practically impossible. The few El Molo who have moved to the mainland near the Catholic mission have more construction materials available. Their houses are much larger and some even have several rooms. One could surmise that if more construction materials were available, the El Molo on the islands would enlarge their present dwellings.

THE EL MOLO ISLAND VILLAGE. Most of all of the present-day El Molo houses are seen in this picture. This barren island is in Lake Rudolph.

SAMBURU

The Samburu range over an area of eleven thousand square miles between Lake Rudolf and the Uaso Nyiro River. Population figures vary, but thirty thousand seems to be the most consistent figure. They are Para-Nilotic, closely related to the Masai of southern Kenya.

The Samburu and Masai once lived side by side, with the Samburu in their present location and the Masai living in the Kenya highlands just south of the Samburu. The British colonialists wanted the highlands for their farms, so they relocated the Masai south of the highlands toward the Tanzania border. A gap of a hundred and fifty miles now separates the two Samburu groups, but they still have similar customs and languages.

The Samburu territory contains several different kinds of environments. The eastern area is low scrub desert with a rainfall of less than ten inches a year. The central and southern area is a higher plateau which receives about twenty inches of rain per year. This region has plenty of grass which offers good feed for the cattle. In the north there are several mountain ranges, and a few Samburu live near the tops of these mountains where there is more rainfall and lush vegetation.

According to Teasdale (oral communication, May 1975), the Samburu do not generally practice agriculture except in some of the higher-altitude areas. They are a pastoral people whose culture revolves around their cattle. These cattle are of the Boran type which are immune to many of the local diseases and are able to live in an adverse climate. A homestead usually has a herd of about eighty cattle. These cattle herds are kept spread out in order for them to get enough grazing and water. The cattle are watered every day during the wet season, but by the end of the dry season they are watered only every third day since it is so far from the water holes to the remaining pasturage. The main diet of the Samburu is milk in different forms, and when the milk is low they will bleed the cows. Sometimes some of the stock is killed for meat, usually the goats and sheep.

There is no private ownership of land, and technically anyone can live where he pleases. There is a tendency for related groups to use specific areas for living and grazing their cattle. Water holes are also commonly held by the tribe, and each herd must wait its turn to drink. If a man digs a well, he then has first rights to that water.

The Samburu tend to live in settlements that are a collection of homesteads arranged in a large circle. Everyone in a settlement is usually related or of the same age set. People in these homesteads assist each other in herding the livestock and in milking. The settlements are usually built near water and salt licks. If the people in the settlements have large herds, they will send the greater portion of the herds away with the young men who will live in cattle camps. A smaller milk herd is kept near the settlement to provide food for the people left at home. The population of these settlements is constantly changing. Periodically the whole settlement is abandoned and a new site is chosen. A thorn fence encircles the whole settlement, and homesteads are built inside the perimeter of this fence. The center of the village is made up of various animal yards

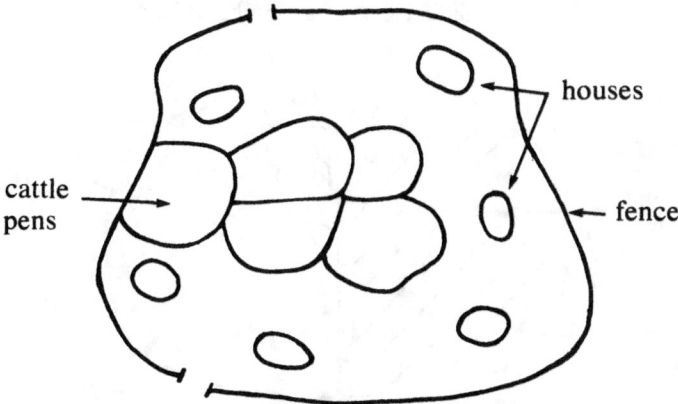

Fig. 33. Samburu settlement (Spencer 1965:18)

for the livestock. A homestead is headed by one stock owner who may have one wife and therefore only one house. If he has plural wives, he will own more houses accordingly, but they are all part of the same homestead.

Each woman has her own house where she lives with her children. These houses are usually oval with a rounded roof. The framework is made by tying sticks together in a basket-like shape, but the outer covering varies from area to area.

In the low desert the houses are moved more often, so they are covered with skins and mats of short grass. Such a house can be disassembled quickly and the mats and skins loaded on a donkey and moved to the next site. These houses are divided into two rooms by donkey packs. The outer room by the door is used for cooking and sitting. The inner room has a raised cowhide that is used for sleeping.

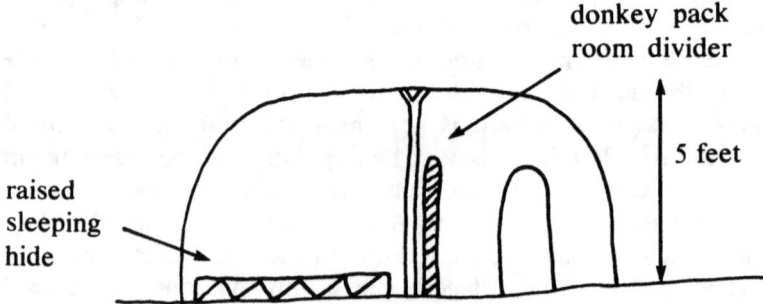

Fig. 34. Side view of a Samburu house

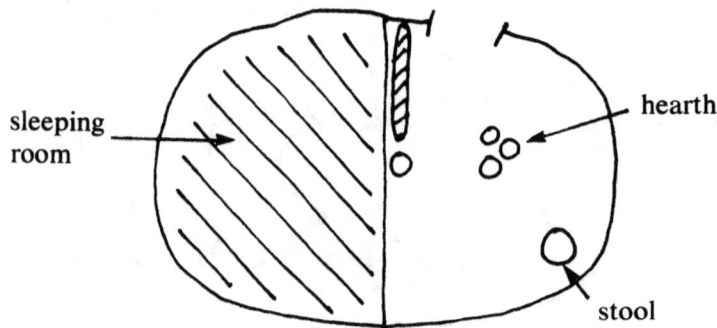

Fig. 35. Layout of a Samburu house (Spencer 1965:18)

Samburu

Forms of the houses in the higher plains are similar. Since pasturage is more plentiful there, the Samburu move less often, so their homes are more permanent. They plaster the outer walls of their houses with cow dung. This not only rainproofs them but gives better insulation from the night cold. Periodically it is necessary to apply a new layer of cow dung when the old layer starts cracking. These houses are often larger than those in the deserts, containing several separate rooms.

The Samburu in the mountains are sedentary, sometimes even practicing a little agriculture. Their houses, built with sturdy cedar logs for the walls, are permanent. These, like the others, have a rounded roof that is periodically replastered with cow dung.

The shape of the Samburu house is an established form that has very little variation from area to area. The environments in which the Samburu live do affect how often the people have to move. This in turn affects the materials which the Samburu use to build these houses. Those who live in a dry climate where they are forced to move often use portable materials, while those in semipermanent sites build more substantial houses plastered with cow dung. Permanent houses in the mountains are built with even more care and are strong and durable.

A SAMBURU DESERT HOUSE. Primarily grass mats cover the stick frames of these desert homes.

MULTIROOMED HIGHLAND HOUSE. Permanent residence makes it practical for Highland Samburu to build large, warm houses.

REPLASTERING THE HOUSE. Highland Samburu plaster their houses with cow dung which dries out and must be patched periodically to keep it intact.

RENDILLE

The Rendille are nomadic and live in the low deserts due south of Mount Marsabit (see fig. 31). Their population probably stands at about thirty thousand. They are linguistically classified in the Somali group.

Somali-speaking peoples number about five million living mostly in Somaliland and Ethiopia. A number of them also live in northeastern Kenya. The Rendille seem to have been an ancient splinter group from the major Somali people. They eventually moved to the central deserts of Kenya and controlled territory as far west as Lake Rudolf. When the Turkana invaded from the west, they forced the Rendille back into their present location.

The Kaisut Desert in which the Rendille live is one of the hottest in Kenya. Temperatures sometimes reach 110° F during the day. The land is a combination of lava and sand deserts. Permanent water sources are scarce, but hardy, deep-rooted acacia bushes grow over much of this area.

The Rendille are warriors who give great importance to age sets. In the past they frequently fought with all the peoples around them except the Samburu, with whom they are close allies. There is no competition between them since the Samburu cattle eat grass, and the Rendille camels browse off the higher foliage. At the present time there is a great deal of intermarriage between the two. The Rendille who intermarry usually adopt the Samburu culture and get involved with raising cattle (oral communication, Cameron, May 1975).

Rendille cannot cultivate crops in the desert, and even cattle are unable to survive since there is little grass in this hostile environment. The Rendille are a camel people who receive their sustenance from the milk and the blood of their camel herds. Camels feed on the leaves of the acacia bushes and are capable of traveling vast distances to find food and water. They can go for many days without water, and they give milk far into the dry season after cattle would have dried up. Rendille do not ride their camels but do use some of them as pack animals when moving their villages. The main purpose of the camel herds is to provide milk and meat.

Camels reproduce slowly, so this limits the growth of prosperity among the Rendille. The bride price is about eight camels which is considered so high that few men have more than one wife. When a man dies, his entire herd is passed on intact to his eldest son. The younger sons do not receive a share and therefore are limited as to their position in the society (Spencer 1965).

Camel herds can move up to forty miles a day finding food and water, so the people herding them must be in good physical condition to stay up with them. The herds are usually split. Larger herds stay on the move with only the healthiest and strongest of the Rendille moving with them. Herders build temporary camps at night, and are often away from water for days at a time. During this time the herders receive all the necessary moisture from the camels' milk. The rest of the Rendille live in settlements of up to a hundred people near a permanent water source. These settlements are groups of homesteads all placed inside the same thorn fence. A small, subsistence herd of milk camels is kept near each settlement to supply food to the inhabitants. Only when the weather gets very dry do the settlements disperse and the people split up to follow their individual camel herds (Spencer 1965).

Rendille houses are almost identical with those of the desert-dwelling Samburu. The environment in which they live offers very little in the way of construction materials. The Rendille drive small sticks into the ground in a circle, then bend these over and tie them at the top, creating a hemisphere. Dried hides and mats of short grass are then tied onto this frame. Near the road and towns, the Rendille use anything at hand, such as burlap, cardboard, and tin to cover their houses. These houses are small—ten feet in diameter and standing only about five feet high. Since building materials are so scarce, these houses are disassembled and moved from one site to another. Even the sticks which make up the frame are taken by donkey to the new house site.

The mobility of the Rendille society causes them to build houses which are quickly constructed and easily moved. Since materials are

Rendille

so scarce, it is of benefit to use portable materials that can be used over and over. Their hemispherical houses also stand up well to the desert winds. Both their way of life and their environment limit the Rendille as to what house form they may choose.

RENDILLE DWELLINGS. Situated among the rocks, the hemispherical houses of the Rendille are similar to those of the desert Samburu.

MOVING DAY. When the Rendille change house sites, they load their precious building material such as goatskins and sticks onto donkeys to transport it to the new location.

CONCLUSION

The indigenous buildings discussed in the preceding sections are constructed in a variety of forms. All of these houses have met the sociocultural and environmental demands of the people who build them. "Housing is shaped by lifestyles, by needs, and, of course, by possibilities" (Gardi 1973:7). There are many different factors which have an impact on house form, and these are often complex. In given situations certain determinants are given primary importance, while in other situations these same determinants may be relegated to a lesser role.

Shelter

A basic purpose of housing is to provide shelter from the elements. Climate is therefore often an important determinant in house form. The climate in the area under study is basically hot, so all houses are built in a manner that will keep them cool. Thick thatch roofs are used to help insulate the house from the sun. Conical roofs also help, since the hot air rises and escapes through the tip of the cone. Windows are never built, so the sun's rays do not enter the house, and although the house interiors are therefore dark, this adds to the coolness. Some indigenous houses are round, and Daniels (1974:48) states that "a round house provides the smallest surface area for the volume enclosed. In a hot, dry zone this form provides the smallest heating area exposed to the sun at any one time."

Houses are also built to provide shelter from the rain. The steep-pitched roofs are excellent for shedding water and keeping the interior of the house dry. Granaries and some houses are built on poles to keep them above the wet ground during the rainy season. The round desert houses are not rainproof, but since it seldom rains this is not a major problem.

In the deserts where strong winds are a problem, hemispherical houses are built rather than cylindrical ones with conical roofs. These structures have no flat surfaces or eaves that can offer resistance to wind flow.

Materials, construction, and technology

Materials, construction, and technology also have an influence on house form. I agree with Rapoport (1968:93) who states that this is not an important factor, but rather a modifying influence. Indigenous people have to build with the construction materials at hand. In southern Sudan and northern Kenya, these materials consist of trees, grass, mud, and sometimes skins. In western Sudan where there is an abundance of trees and grass, these materials are not an important factor in deciding house form. There are certain structural limits to what can be built, but within these limitations are many possible variations of house styles.

Construction materials place greater limitations on house forms where they are scarce, since they then limit the options available. In the deserts where both trees and grass are rare, the lack of materials causes the people to build small houses of sticks and hides. A scarcity of building materials limits the possible variety in house styles. This is especially true of a group like the El Molo.

The technology of all these peoples is basically the same. A framework for the walls is made by pushing sticks or poles into the ground, outlining the desired size and shape of the building. Then horizontal sticks are interwoven or tied into these with bark to provide strength. This framework is covered with various materials such as mud, grass, palm fronds, or hides. All of the houses fit into two basic types of construction. The first has a steeply pitched roof set on the walls or directly on the ground, and the other is hemispherical. Within this limited technology it is possible to come up with many variations in house form, so technology has little bearing on which form is actually chosen.

Conclusion

Defense

Protection from wildlife and from warring groups is a need felt by many of the people living in this region, so defense is an important determinant. Houses are strongly built and sometimes elevated to protect the inhabitants from predatory animals and snakes. Among warring groups, the people build stockades, thorn fences, archways, lookout towers, and low doors all for defense against attack.

Site

Housing sites are chosen for physical and environmental reasons. Agricultural people traditionally place their houses in the midst of their fields near a permanent water supply. Villages recently built along the roads, however, are breaking with this pattern. The Bongo try to place their homesteads around a large tree which will shade much of the living space. Those who live in the flood plains place their permanent houses on higher ground that never floods, and build only temporary shelters in areas that are often under water. Site is especially important for groups like the Didinga who build their homesteads on precarious ledges for defense. Although site is important to all the people, only in rare cases does it actually have a direct impact on the house form itself.

Social factors

Each society has its own unique culture, and within this milieu are various social demands that have an important impact on house form. Oliver (1969:27) states that living space must serve social functions. This is true in the area under study where often "form appears to be more 'culturally' than 'climatically' oriented" (Obot 1974:84).

In all groups practicing polygamy, although two or more women may have the same husband, each has the right to her own house. Each wife therefore has her own private domain and is expected not to interfere with the others. Difference in social status is a factor in the house form that is used. Among the Zande, for instance, the man builds a big, mud-walled house for his first wife, but the succeeding wives usually receive a bell-shaped grass house. Positioning of a house can also be a result of social status. Among the Murle, the senior wife places her house in the northeast section of the cluster, the position of prominence.

All of the peoples under study build houses for the integral family unit, but also feel a need for close companionship with other people. These peoples, therefore, build their houses around a central courtyard where much of the daily activity takes place. The Highland Murle, Toposa, and Didinga build special community sitting areas for people to meet and talk. The famine situation of the Ik has reversed this system for them. They build private compounds with the doors facing outwards so no sharing of food is necessary; however, they still share a common sitting place outside the settlement.

Whether people live together in large villages or are scattered in small homesteads depends on social reasons. The Bongo are afraid of evil spells, so they live as far from the neighboring homestead as possible. They build their houses without assistance, which results in their being small. By comparison, the Lotuko enjoy human companionship and group together for defense in large fortified villages. The people cooperate to build stockades, cattle kraals, and towers. Where they assist each other in building, this results in larger, better-built dwellings.

Subsistence focus

A people's subsistence focus is strongly influenced by the environment in which they live. People have to eat, and the way they procure their food is largely a matter of the environment in which they live. The environment may influence them to stay in one location and grow crops, or cause them to move frequently in order to hunt or to find enough grazing for their livestock. House forms therefore have to be adapted to fit a subsistence focus.

Agriculturalists all build permanent, substantial houses. Since a house will be used for a long time, much effort and work are put into building it. The framework and walls are strongly built, and the thatching is carefully done. There are often several variations in house styles being used in the same area. Agriculturalists need to store their crops, so elevated granaries are built to keep grain dry until needed. All of the agricultural people in the area under study build similar round, conical-roofed houses unless outside forces have intervened.

The pure nomads all build small, hemispherical houses. These people must keep moving in order to survive, and most of their time and effort is spent caring for their livestock. Their houses are hastily constructed and materials are often portable. One particular house

Conclusion   123

form is used because this has proved to be the most efficient. When some of these nomadic people do settle in a permanent location, such as the Samburu on Mount Kulal, they build larger houses and often do change the house form.

The seminomads of central and eastern Sudan build both permanent and temporary houses. Permanent villages are built in locations above the flood level, so the houses are large and durable. Herdsmen spend much of the time far from the village following the grazing cattle. These herdsmen build temporary shelters which are hastily constructed and follow no set form.

The major hypothesis of this study is that house forms are a reflection of subsistence focus. This hypothesis applies in fifteen of the tribes under discussion. The Highland Murle and El Molo at first seem to be exceptions, but in both cases there are special circumstances that explain the divergence from the norm.

Culture change and contact

People learn by coming in contact with various ways of doing things. In looking at the area under discussion from west to east, one can see a gradual change in house forms. Starting with round, conical-roofed houses in the west, there is a shift to hemispherical houses in the east. Houses are not radically different from one tribe to the next since the people borrow positive ideas on house form from those with whom they are in contact.

History can have an important impact on house form. When the turmoil in western Sudan (1850–1900) changed the cultures of many smaller groups, they gradually adopted new customs. Their house styles changed from the traditional round houses to the newly introduced rectangular ones. The Zande are another example of how history has influenced house forms. Present Zande house forms are a direct result of their conquests and absorption of others. These house styles are a combination of many cultures. When the British forced the Zande to move out of the bush into large villages, this also had a direct impact on their house styles. The Murle, who moved to their present location by way of a long migration, have kept an oral history of their travels. Their four major stops are displayed in the placement of their houses within the homesteads.

Recent events such as government intervention can also be a factor in changing house styles. As long as the Ik were hunters, they built small igloo-shaped houses. When the government prohibited hunting and forced them to live in a permanent location, they immediately dropped their old house forms and adopted those of their new neighbors.

Language

The hypothesis that language and house form are interrelated is invalid. The language spoken has nothing to do with house forms. It is possible to find groups that are closely related linguistically, but who have totally different house styles. The Lotuko, Toposa, Turkana, and Samburu are all Para-Nilotic, but their houses are all different. The same is true of the Murle and the Didinga who are closely related linguistically but whose houses have few similarities. There are also peoples such as the Shatt and the Bongo who are totally unrelated linguistically but have similar cultures and house styles. Languages are practical in showing relationships and origins, but are not a factor in the choice of actual house styles.

Summary

A house must meet the sociocultural demands of the builder and be an adequate shelter in the specific environment in which it is built. Many house forms could be built from the available materials that would meet these requirements. A society decides on a certain form not only because it meets its requirements, but also because it likes a certain style. The ultimate choice of what form to use is as complex as the many factors that enter into this decision.

APPENDIX

Communications cited

1. Ahad
   An ex-policeman from the Nuba mountains who has settled on the Boma plateau. He has married a Murle woman, speaks the Murle language fluently, and has a thorough knowledge of their culture.

2. Cameron, Louise
   A nurse with the Africa Inland Mission who has spent a number of years working with the Samburu and Rendille. She is constantly gathering new linguistic and cultural data on the Rendille.

3. Didinga headmaster
   A man from the Didinga tribe who is presently head of the school at Chukudum. He has relatives living in the remote part of the hills, and therefore is still in contact with the traditional customs.

4. Didinga teacher
   A teacher from the Didinga tribe who has spent most of his life around Chukudum.

5. Father John
   A Bongo who has recently become a Catholic priest. He has been working among his own people starting primary schools

in the bush. He took us on a personal tour of the Bongo area before leaving for further studies in Rome.

6. Kparabatiko, Philip
    A Zande who is presently in charge of education in the Tambura area. He has written a history of the Zande tribe which has been published in Italian under another name.

7. Mangayat chief
    Government-assigned leader of the Mangayat. He has recently taken a census of the members of his community.

8. Mvuni, Nikoli
    One of the heads of the Africa Inland Church in Sudan. He is a Madi, but has been working at Torit among the Lotuko for several years.

9. Parr, Peter
    As a missionary's son he spent several years at Pibor Post among the Murle during the late 1950s. He is presently a member of an agricultural project in Sudan.

10. Shatt chief
    Present chief of the Shatt who is proud of their heritage and customs.

11. Teasdale, Paul
    Head of the Africa Inland Mission in northern Kenya. He is a missionary's son raised in Kenya and has a good understanding of customs in this part of Kenya.

12. Toposa teacher
    A Toposa who teaches at a village school near Kapoeta. He has lived all of his life in this area.

13. Trader
    A Murle who buys coffee on the Boma plateau and sells it in Pibor Post.

14. Tucker, A. N.
    The leading linguist for northeast African languages. He is

presently retired in England where I had personal discussions with him in Oct. 1974 and July 1975.

15. Wapuwa, Joseph

    The main chief of the Longarim. He has received a high-school education and speaks excellent English. He is personally involved in trying to better the lives of his people by bringing in education, medicine, and agriculture.

16. Wilson, Steve

    A builder from the Africa Inland Mission who is building a fishery for the Shangilla at Iluret. He was born and raised in Kenya and has a good grasp of Swahili and the cultures in northern Kenya.

BIBLIOGRAPHY

References cited

Barbour, K.M. 1961. *The Republic of the Sudan: A Regional Geography*. London: University of London Press.

Bicknell, Peter. 1972. Zande Savagery. In Andre Singer (ed.), *Zande Themes*, pp. 41–63.

Cohen, D.W. 1968. The River-Lake Nilotes from the Fifteenth to the Nineteenth Century. In B.A. Ogot (ed.), *Zimani: A Survey of East African History*, pp. 142–57.

Daniels, Greg. 1974. An Indigenous Response to Building in Developing Countries. *Shelter in Developing Countries*. U.C.L.A.

de Blij, Harm J. 1964. *A Geography of Subsaharan Africa*. Chicago: Rand McNally and Co.

Deng, Francis Mading. 1972. *The Dinka of the Sudan*. New York: Holt, Rinehart, and Winston.

Dickens, Sherry. 1974. Cultural Influences on Materials and Methods. *Shelter in Developing Countries*, pp. 23–31. U.C.L.A.

Driberg, J.H. 1930. *People of the Small Arrow*. New York: Payson and Clarke.

Ehret, Christopher. 1971. Cushites and the Highland and Plains Nilotes. In B.A. Ogot (ed.), *Zamani*, pp. 158–76.

Evans-Pritchard, E.E. 1940. *The Nuer*. Oxford: Clarendon Press.

———. 1971. *The Azande*. Oxford: Clarendon Press.

———. 1974. *Man and Woman among the Azande*. London: Faber and Faber.

Fraser, Douglas. 1968. *Village Planning in the Primitive World*. New York: George Braziller.

Gardi, Rene. 1973. *Indigenous African Architecture*. Bern: Van Nostrand Reinhold Co.

Greenberg, J.H. 1963. *Languages of Africa*. The Hague: Indiana University and Mouton.

Gulliver, Pamela and P.H. 1953. *The Central Nilo-Hamites*. London: B.P.C. Letterpress. [Reprint 1968.]

Gulliver, P.H. 1955. *The Family Herds*. Westport, Conn.: Negro Universities Press. [Reprint 1970.]

Hodgkin, Robin A. 1951. *Sudan Geography*. Great Britain: Longmans, Green, and Co.

Jackson, H.C. 1955. *Behind the Modern Sudan*. London: Macmillan and Co.

Jackson, John B. 1961. Essential Architecture. *Landscape* 10:3:27–30.

Lewis, B.A. 1972. *The Murle*. Oxford: Clarendon Press.

Nalder, L.F. (ed.). 1937. *A Tribal Survey of Mangalla Province*. Oxford University Press.

Nelson, Harold D. 1973. *Area Handbook for the Democratic Republic of Sudan*. Washington, D.C.: U.S. Government Printing Office.

Bibliography

Obot, Isaiah. 1974. Settlement Pattern and House Form Determinants. *Shelter in Developing Countries*, pp. 82–88. U.C.L.A.

Ogot, B.A. and J.A. Kieran (eds.). 1971. *Zamani: A Survey of East African History*. East African Publishing House and Longmans.

Oliver, Paul (ed.). 1969. *Shelter and Society*. New York: Frederick A. Praeger.

Prussin, Labelle. 1969. *Architecture in Northern Ghana: A Study of Forms and Functions*. Berkeley and Los Angeles: University of California Press.

Rapoport, Amos. 1969. *House Form and Culture*. Englewood Cliffs: Prentice-Hall.

Santandrea, S. 1953. An Account of the Indri, Togoyo, Feroge, etc. *Sudan Notes and Records* 34:230–64.

———. 1968. *The Luo of the Bahr El Ghazal*. Italy: delle Missioni Africane de Verona.

Schweinfurth, Georg. 1874. *The Heart of Africa*. New York: Harper and Brothers.

———. 1875. *Artes Africanae*. London: Sampson Low, Marston, Low, and Searle.

Seligman, C.G. and Brenda Z. Seligman. 1932. *Pagan Tribes of the Nilotic Sudan*. London: George Routledge and Sons.

Singer, Andre and Brian Street (eds.). 1972. *Zande Themes*. New Jersey: Rowman and Littlefield.

Spencer, Paul. 1965. *The Samburu*. Los Angeles: University of California Press.

Sudan Survey Department. 1974. *Vegetation of Sudan*. Map printed in Khartoum.

Sutton, J.E.G. 1968. The Settlement of East Africa. In B.A. Ogot (ed.), *Zimani*, pp. 69–99.

Tucker, A.N. and M.A. Bryan. 1956. *The Non-Bantu Languages of North-Eastern Africa*. London: Oxford University Press.

Turnbull, Colin M. 1972. *The Mountain People*. New York: Simon and Schuster.

Walton, James. 1956. *African Village*. Pretoria: J.L. Van Schaik.

Sources consulted

Adamson, Joy. 1967. *The Peoples of Kenya*. London: Collins and Harvill Press.

Albino, Oliver. 1970. *The Sudan: A Southern Viewpoint*. London: Oxford University Press.

Austin, H.H. 1902. *Among Swamps and Giants in Equatorial Africa*. London: C. Arthur Pearson.

Baker, Samuel. 1866. *Albert Nyanza: Great Basin of the Nile*, 2 Vols. New York: Macmillan and Co.

———. 1874. *Ismailia*. New York: Harper and Brothers.

Carde, R. Scott. 1974. Kenya and Tanzania: Population Dynamics and Housing. *Shelter in Developing Countries*, pp. 97–103. U.C.L.A.

Cerulli, Ernesta. 1956. *Peoples of South-West Ethiopia and Its Border-Land*. London: Hazell, Watson, and Viney.

Cookson, John A. 1964. *United States Area Handbook for the Republic of the Sudan*. Washington, D.C.: Foreign Areas Studies.

Cunnison, Ian and Wendy James (eds.). 1972. *Essays in Sudan Ethnography*. London: C. Hurst and Company.

Bibliography

Eprile, Cecil. 1974. *War and Peace in the Sudan: 1955-1972*. London: David and Charles.

Hillaby, John. 1964. *Journey to the Jade Sea*. London: Constable and Co.

Huntingford, G.W.B. 1953. *The Northern Nilo-Hamites*. London: B.P.C. Letterpress.

———. 1955. *The Galla of Ethiopia: The Kingdoms of Kafa and Janjero*. London: Lowe and Brydone.

Junker, Wilhelm. 1890-92. *Travels in Africa*, 3 Vols. London: Chapman and Hall.

Knuffel, Werner E. 1973. *The Construction of the Bantu Grass Hut*. Graz, Austria: Akademische Druck u. Verlagsanstalt.

Kronenberg, Andreas and Waltraud Kronenberg. 1972. The Bovine Idiom and Formal Logic. In Cunnison and James (eds.), *Essays in Sudan Ethnography*.

Lewis, I.M. 1955. *Peoples of the Horn of Africa*. London: Hazell, Watson, and Viney.

Ludwig, Emil. 1937. *The Nile*. New York: The Viking Press.

Moorehead, Alan. 1960. *The White Nile*. London: Hamish Hamilton.

Ogot, B.A. 1967. *History of the Southern Luo*. East African Publishing House.

Ojany, Francis F. 1968. The Geography of East Africa. In B.A. Ogot (ed.), *Zimani*, pp. 22-48.

Oliver, Paul (ed.). 1971. *Shelter in Africa*. London: Barrie and Jenkins.

Ominde, S.H. (ed.). 1971. *Studies in East African Geography and Development*. Berkeley and Los Angeles: University of California Press.

Petherick. 1869. *Travels in Central Africa*, 2 Vols. London: Tinsley Brothers.

Rayne, H. 1923. *The Ivory Raiders*. London: William Heinemann.

Riefenstall, Leni and Max Planck Institute, Munich. 1973. *The Last of the Nuba*. New York: Harper and Row.

Smith, A. Donaldson. 1897. *Through Unknown African Countries*. Edward Arnold.

Stigand, C.H. 1923. *Equatoria, The Lado Enclave*. Constable and Co.

Thomas, Elizabeth Marshall. 1965. *Warrior Herdsman*. Alfred A. Knopf.

Tuan, Yi-Fu. 1974. *Topophilia*. Englewood Cliffs, N.J.: Prentice Hall.

Tucker, A.N. 1931. The Tribal Confusion around Wau. *Sudan Notes and Records* 14:49–60.

———— and M.A. Bryan. 1966. *Linguistical Analysis, The Non-Bantu Languages of North-Eastern Africa*. Oxford Press.

Vansina, Jan. 1961. *Oral Tradition*. Chicago: Adline Publishing.

Whitehead, G.O. 1953. "Suppressed Classes Among the Bari and Bari-Speaking Tribes," *Sudan Notes and Records* 34.

Wyndham, Richard. 1936. *The Gentle Savage*. London: Cassell and Company, Ltd.

www.ingramcontent.com/pod-product-compliance
Lightning Source LLC
Chambersburg PA
CBHW051813230426
43672CB00012B/2725